SWIMMING WITH COBRAS

Publication © Modjaji Books 2011
Copyright © Rosemary Smith 2011

First published in 2011 by Modjaji Books PTY Ltd
P O Box 385, Athlone, 7760, South Africa
modjaji.books@gmail.com
http://modjaji.book.co.za
www.modjajibooks.co.za

ISBN 978-1-920397-37-1

Book design: Natascha Mostert
Cover artwork and lettering: Jesse Breytenbach
Printed and bound by Mega Digital, Cape Town
Set in Palatino

Acknowledgements

This book has had a long gestation period, culled as it is from the diaries I kept since arriving in South Africa in 1966. Throughout this long period I have incurred many debts to friends both in Grahamstown and England, to the many Black Sashers who inspired and nurtured me, and to the mainly Eastern Cape people whom I met through my work who showed me a depth of humanity I did not know existed.

There are too many people to name and thank individually but as in my dedication I must name a few. Firstly I thank Colleen Higgs and Mojadji Books who had faith enough to publish the book. Secondly Karen Robertson who was the editor and made all the editing sessions interesting and fun! Without these two people the book would never have seen the light of day. William Barnes in London was a meticulous and kind encourager of early drafts. Sadly, he died shortly before the book was published. And to Lynette Paterson, who put in swathes of time prodding, pushing and suggesting, my debt is enormous.

Finally, the love and encouragement of my husband Malvern and children Matthew, Anna, Charlotte and Lucy has sustained me throughout and I am deeply grateful to them.

Rosemary Smith

SWIMMING WITH COBRAS
Rosemary Smith

For William who began it all.

For the family who lived it.

And for Lynette, without whom it would not have come to fruition.

Rosemary Smith

"The pattern of women's lives lies ... locked in old diaries, stuffed away in old drawers."

– *Virginia Woolf, 1929*

arbitrarily if
...lowed
...s - candidates
...f English
...phrasing their
...e the ideal
...ely

...stance a chief
...o act when
...cies in ideal
...ointed out.
...DET is attempting
... kinds of difficul-
...ove by introducing
... examination pa-
...e, last year a multi-
...r was used in the
...re matriculation ex-
...is development re-
... investigation to
...r alia whether or not
... being further disad-

...ack Sash education
...p

hardly a dry eye as all the delegates linked arms and sang 'We shall overcome' and consensus was reached that apartheid must go.

The disadvantage of such a diverse group was that it was hard to get some of the discussion focused and in some instances to get beyond the superficial. There was an emphasis on mothers rather than attempts to formulate shared oppression. Perhaps the greatest value came in the de-mythologising on both sides and in the words of one of the ANC women, Frene Ginwala, 'In the three days of discussion a chink has opened the barriers between us. This has been a two-way process and our understanding has been enhanced through the exchange of our personal experiences.'

Rosie Smith

Braklaagte banning

The Transvaal Rural Action Committee, a subcommittee of the Black Sash, was banned from Bophuthatswana after exposing an outbreak of violence in the twin villages of Braklaagte and Leeuwfontein.

Early in July, nine policemen an... two villagers were killed in clashe... after Bophuthatswana police had i... tervened in a protest against t... incorporation of the two villages i... the 'homeland'.

The Bophuthatswana governm... has accused the Black Sash and ... of instigating the revolt and of b... 'engaged in activities which ... danger the national security or p... safety'.

The Black Sash's respons... been: 'We have not created ... conditions, we have merely e... them. Banning the Black Sa... not mean opposition will c... exist.'

Rosemary van Wyk-Smith addressing the conference

...conference,
...e

... the IDASA conference
... in the Struggle for Peace' in
... in April was exciting and
...ging but above all one felt as
... one was encapsulated in a big
...nal bubble. For 55 women
...South Africa to meet with 25
... African exiles from the ANC
...ons around the world, the ex-
...ce was bound to be charged
...motion.

...e South African delegation was
...sparate one both in terms of
...grounds and political traditions
...h proved to be both ad-
...ageous and disadvantageous.
... advantage was that one felt this
... a reaching out, a conscientising
... some women who barely knew
...ir fellow South Africans and had
...viously stereotyped the ANC. At
...ference there was

Women in the struggle for peace in Harare

Contents

Introduction	ii
Swimming with cobras	1
A sheltered life	9
Not a person	21
Establishing an identity	32
Working days	49
Time out	69
Repression hits the Eastern Cape	80
More detentions	96
Getting the message across	112
Chinks appearing	125
Improvements in progress	136
Knitting with barbed wire	150
At home	160

Introduction

It was the summer of 1961. I was in my mid-twenties, living a blissfully sheltered life in Oxford, England. I'd just met Malvern van Wyk Smith, the Rhodes scholar from South Africa whom I would one day marry, unaware that in just five years' time I would land on the shores of his homeland, destined for the small university town of Grahamstown – a stranger in an even stranger land.

I arrived in 1966 when South Africa had been a republic for five years and Nelson Mandela had been on Robben Island for two. The widespread civil disobedience campaigns of the 1950s and early 1960s had been forcefully suppressed and almost the entire leadership of the liberation movement was either in exile, in prison or banned. In September of my first year in Grahamstown, the architect of apartheid, Hendrik Verwoerd, was stabbed to death on the floor of parliament and the system's enforcer, John Vorster, became the country's fourth Nationalist Prime Minister. Twenty-eight years of turmoil lay ahead.

Realising that the timing of my arrival had placed me in the midst of momentous events, I began a book of jottings. History no longer belonged exclusively to the eminent and the great, and I sensed that as a woman making a new life in an alien land I would have a story to tell. At first my thoughts were dominated by the overwhelming feeling of contrast with my previous life. Then as I became more settled I began to write down events, conversations or observations that intrigued or startled me. In 1968, prompted by the intelligent and lively women who were actively engaged in the struggle to right the wrongs of the society I found myself in, I joined the local branch of the Black Sash, a white, women-led anti-apartheid organisation. By 1970, Malvern and I had four small children and my diaries became scraps of paper or scribbles in notebooks as I recorded events in the snatched time between domestic chores and Sash meetings. In the mid-1980s, when the spectre of detention hovered over me, I took the precaution of putting the diaries into a plastic packet in an ice cream container in the deep freeze!

Turning to those fragments, I realise how much has been erased from my memory and how much passed me by because, at the time, I was unable to grasp the context. I am also aware that much has been, and will be, written by people who played far more central roles in South Africa's struggle for liberation. My part in the events I am recalling was a small one. And yet, living in a town in the Eastern Cape during the apartheid years, a seething microcosm of the larger South Africa, I had opportunities to witness events at close range. I participated in widely divergent activities and communities, and my work over several decades took me in and out of the beleaguered townships, something often denied city dwellers. And so, while my life has not been extraordinary, my vantage point has been a privileged one. In the pages that follow, I have unlocked my diaries and pulled open the drawers of my life, to shine a light on a small, but important, slice of South African history.

Swimming with cobras

Eastern Cape rivers are not like the English trout streams of my childhood where the clear water sparkles and rushes over smooth pebbles. They are often sluggish, the water a murky brown masking the river bed beneath.

One hot, late-summer day, after hiking in the veld with friends, wary of the little pepper ticks clinging to the tall grass waiting for their moment to jump onto our warm bodies, we came upon a tree house. It was guarded by a ficus tree, the giant roots gnarled into a solid buttress. And from a wide platform, it looked out upon towering cliffs. The folds of rock reminded me that millions of years ago the sea had swept over this landscape. Now it was covered with antique cycads that looked like pineapple tops, and splodges of light blue plumbago and orange tacoma trembling in clouds of white butterflies. The cliffs were home to several families of baboons who heckled us from their vantage point, their rough barks echoing off the rocks.

Below the tree house, the upper reaches of the Kariega River formed a wide and full stream, perfect for swimming. The water danced with flashes of colour in the late sunlight – greens, earth browns, golds and coppers inviting us, hot and dusty from our hike, to plunge in. Lying on my back in the water, reflecting on the day's walk through virtually untouched countryside, I thought of a line from Yeats' poem *The Lake Isle of Innisfree*, where in a "bee-loud glade" peace came "dropping slow." My reverie was disturbed by cries from my fellow swimmers as a flash of coppery yellow caught my eye.

"Snake!" someone shouted. A cobra was swimming beside us, his long body curving and undulating.

"Snake in the water!" Everyone made for the bank and scrambled out of the river. I grabbed at the roots of an overhanging tree, heaving and pushing against the mud of the bank, slipping in my attempts to gain purchase, panicking until I got to the top. Legs covered in mud, heart beating furiously, I looked back to see the cobra swimming mid-stream, unconcerned by the commotion. There was no flickering forked tongue, just a purposeful, sinuous swim. Except for this movement, one might have mistaken it for a stick, so well was it camouflaged in the dappled water.

As I lay in my sleeping bag that night, I thought of my many walks in the green storybook hills of the English countryside; such a contrast to Africa where the hillsides that beckoned were often deceiving, turning out to be rough and treacherous, with rocky cliffs and prickly bush. Here the dappled water could stir at any moment with sinister life. Here, in the most peaceful moments, danger was never far away.

With hindsight I realised the unprovoked cobra was nothing to fear. Still, its coppery flash remained with me, lurking alongside many of my experiences in my adopted country. Years later as I sat in a Port Elizabeth township hall with peeling walls and broken toilets, watching the notorious South African Police commander, Eugene de Kock, testify before the Truth and Reconciliation Commission (TRC), I thought of it again. With his dark, heavy spectacles De Kock seemed to me the embodiment of evil. Descriptions of Vlakplaas, the bushveld farm where apartheid hit squads were trained, conjured up monstrous scenes from Dante's *Inferno*. Except that the testimony of De Kock's colleague Dirk Coetzee on the burning of the body of anti-apartheid activist Sizwe Kondile at Vlakplaas in 1981 was like no poem I had ever read. "The burning of a body on an open fire takes seven hours. While that happened we were drinking and braaing next to the fire... The fleshier pieces take longer, that's why we frequently had to turn the buttocks and thighs." I thought of others nearer home whose remains had suffered a similar fate and I wanted to throw up. Yet if I had seen De Kock or Coetzee on the street, would there have been any clue to their pasts? Torturers bear no mark of Cain; hit squad men giving testimony in suits and ties appear innocuous – someone's father or son. Time and again during the TRC hearings, I was struck by what the political theorist and holocaust survivor Hannah Arendt described as "the banality of evil".

Eugene de Kock was one of almost 8 000 people to apply to the TRC for amnesty for human rights violations perpetrated under apartheid. Full disclosure was a prerequisite for amnesty to be granted. Some 22 000 statements were received from victims of atrocities, approximately 2 200 of which were heard in public over a period of two years from April 1996.

In preparation for these hearings, the Black Sash meticulously perused its records of apartheid abuses in the period from March 1960 to May 1994. Our task was to identify people who could apply for reparation and some who might be asked to give their testimony before the commission. It was taxing work for our researchers, sifting through the masses of material and selecting cases based on legislation defined by the Promotion of National Unity and Reconciliation Act of 1995. The emotional cost of reading through the details of assault, torture, murder, deprivation and fear, especially in the 80s during the height of atrocities in the Eastern Cape, gave us all a great deal of empathy for the commissioners.

As we began to hold preliminary interviews with those identified by our research, we listened to hideous reminders of those traumatic years. We had to prepare each interviewee for the process of taking their story to the TRC, as well as offer counsel in terms of their expectations. In particular it was necessary to explain that reparation was likely to be symbolic rather than substantive, and that if amnesty were granted to perpetrators, no prosecution could follow. We did wonder how much agony and bitterness the commission might unleash, but we supported it as a necessary process and certainly one that felt to us like the culmination of the work we had been doing over decades.

Antjie Krog points out in her book, *Country of my Skull*, that the alternative to the TRC would have had to be punitive trials such as those of Nuremberg and Tokyo. Unlike post-war Germany and Japan, however, whose defeats had been complete, post-liberation South Africa faced a situation more like the one in post-Pinochet Chile. The overthrown regime formed part of the new government and continued to have some political power and influence. Furthermore the process of negotiation in this country had established a mood for reconciliation, and so South Africa looked to the Chilean model of a truth commission instead.

Not everyone supported the TRC. In fact, it was often more lauded outside South Africa than within. There were South Africans we knew who showed no interest in reports on the hearings. "It's all over now," they would say. "Why do we have to go back?" Somehow it was the outside world that saw most clearly how miraculous it was that there had been no violent revolution or apocalyptic backlash in this country.

I attended several of these emotionally fraught hearings in Eastern Cape towns, each time reliving the horror of events that the Black Sash had monitored, and meeting up with victims whose stories I, and my fellow Sashers, knew so well.

One such hearing took place in February 1997 in the town of Cradock, once home to Olive Schreiner, the 19th century pacifist, feminist and author of *The Story of an African Farm*. It was also the birthplace of the renowned writer, Guy Butler, who played such a leading role in the English-speaking community that had become my adopted milieu. It was home, too, to activist and community leader Matthew Goniwe, one of the Cradock Four who had disappeared while returning from a meeting in Port Elizabeth in 1985. His badly burnt body, together with those of his comrades, was found near the PE suburb of Blue Water Bay. Nine years later, during a 1994 inquest, we heard how orders had been given for two of the four men to be "permanently removed from society". All four were stopped at a roadblock and brutally killed before their car and their bodies were set on fire. On the day of their funeral, President PW

Botha declared a State of Emergency. Later, Nelson Mandela would say: "The death of these gallant freedom fighters marked a turning point in the history of our struggle. No longer could the regime govern in the old way. They were the true heroes of the struggle."

That hot summer's day, the Cradock town hall was full of people both young and old. A lighted candle focused the eye and gave a religious air to the proceedings. Each morning it was lit in a simple ceremony to mark the upholding of the truth and the burning of the past. The hall was very still. The commissioners sat on the stage and opposite their table sat the victims, telling their stories and responding to careful questioning. Through our headphones we listened to the translators in their glass cabins. Only here and there did we see a white face.

One of the stories told that day was of a couple who had been banished to nearby Illinge from another Karoo town because of the husband's political activism. In Illinge, living in makeshift accommodation far from family and home, they endured constant police harassment. They were followed when they went out and were often awoken in the dead of night by police raids. People became wary of the strangers in their midst. Small wonder then that when this couple's baby died, there was no money to buy a coffin or have a proper funeral. So we heard about the three-month-old infant placed in a cardboard box and the procession to the cemetery, where with hands and a spade, the parents dug a grave in the hard, drought-ravished soil. As the testifying mother began to keen, a counsellor put an arm around her shoulders until her sobbing ceased. A murmuring, a sighing, rose from the people sitting around us.

Up and down the length and breadth of South Africa, similar scenes played themselves out in dusty halls as the cruel minutiae of life during apartheid spilled out. I was filled with sadness and humility as we stepped out later into the Cradock sun filtering through the feathery pepper trees. So often people would say that all they wanted to know from the commission was where their loved ones had been buried. Just to have a proper grave dug, a headstone erected – such a small request in the face of the tragedies that had wrecked their lives. Eastern Cape poet Mzi Mahola felt their heartache when he wrote in his poem *The Land Will Heal*: "For too long their hearts quivered with grief / As they searched for the vanished / The dead in graves with no holes."

In seeking and recording the truth, the TRC hoped to exorcise shameful events, heal some of the hurt and restore the moral order of society. Noble aims, but how difficult it must have been for the commissioners to sit day after day listening to horror stories unfold. In the first stanza of her poem *The Archbishop Chairs the First Session*, Ingrid de Kok captures the emotion of those sessions in a simple and iconic image:

> On the first day
> after a few hours of testimony
> the Archbishop wept.
> He put his grey head
> on the long table
> of papers and protocols
> and he wept.

It was hard to see, as we listened to story upon story of brutality, beatings and torture, how victims and perpetrators could ever become reconciled. And yet, miraculous tales of forgiveness and hope were commonplace.

We heard that day in Cradock of two families, the one brutalised by the other, who had made peace and now worshipped as members of the same church congregation. In a hearing in East London, another story of forgiveness emerged, of the Kohl family whose teenage son Alistair had been killed by a police bullet 12 years earlier, at the first funeral I'd ever attended in a Grahamstown township.

At the height of the struggle in the 1980s there seemed to be a political funeral every weekend, and each one spawned the next. Typically, in a volatile face-off between young angry activists and nervous soldiers, something would go wrong. Tear gas might be fired into the procession of mourners, people would scatter, aggression would ensue, and before long real bullets, some of which hit innocent people like Alistair, would follow.

This event had irrevocably changed the Kohls' lives, yet they spoke without bitterness or rancour. They listened to others telling similar stories or worse, and later described the hearing as an experience of healing. For my part, I was filled with admiration for this calm, eloquent couple sustained by their strong faith. I had a son of Alistair's age, and not for the first time the truth of the isiXhosa saying, *"Umuntu ngumntu ngobantu"*, became a little clearer for me: a person is a person through other people.

As the Kohls recounted the events that led to Alistair's death, I could feel again the heat, the dust, the pressing crowd and the fear that was so common at these gatherings. The smells and sounds were vivid in my mind, as visceral as the memory of the cobra in the river.

Grahamstown funerals always seemed to be enveloped in a dusty, ash-gritty wind. The acrid smell of smoke from frequent fires on the hillsides around the town clung to our nostrils and sometimes, a thin layer of ash settled on the yellow security vehicles patrolling the streets. It truly seemed as if our society was on fire.

There was no shade in the usually packed football stadium on top of the hill in Joza, one of the three local townships. Skin parched in the sun and dust. Police helicopters buzzed overhead. From time to time we would hear the thud of a tear gas canister as it hit the ground and people would put handkerchiefs to their mouths as an ominous grey cloud floated over the stadium wall.

The mourning family huddled in black by the coffin, often looking rather startled at the hijacking of the funeral for a political purpose. Marshals and speakers sported Cuban-style khaki shirts and black berets. Young men carrying sawn-off pieces of wood fashioned like AK47s danced to the rhythm of the toyi-toyi: knees up, boots thumping, voices chanting "huss-huss". "An injury to one is an injury to all!" the crowd called, and then they sang choruses full of invective, fists raised and clenched in the air. "The cart with no wheels: move, Botha, you're going to be crushed!" or "Mrs Botha is sterile, she gives birth to rats; Mrs Mandela is fertile, she gives birth to comrades!" More chilling would be cries like, "Informers we will kill you, hayi! hayi! Witches we will burn you, hayi! hayi!" But by contrast there would also be the resonantly harmonised hymns and songs, rendered with the pathos and yearning of American negro spirituals. "Freedom is in your hands, show us the way to freedom, let us get away from slavery in this land of Africa."

Whenever possible the Black Sash had representatives at these funerals, who would invariably be asked to give a message. I never minded standing in front of large gatherings, but I often felt my message was tight and pallid in contrast to the full-throated deliveries of the main speakers. I was also ashamed of my linguistic poverty. Proceedings were usually in isiXhosa, yet they were always meticulously interpreted for the handful of non-isiXhosa speakers present. There would be some leaders from the churches in town, some students, perhaps someone from a white opposition party. Our presence was a gesture of solidarity with the embattled and mourning community. The Black Sash was also there to monitor and record events. If things went wrong, there had to be witnesses. And perhaps the presence of a few white pastors and women wearing sashes did act as a restraining factor.

By the time of the TRC I had lived more than 30 years in South Africa. Looking back, as the process forced us all to do, I was sometimes astonished at the experiences I had had, and I was in no doubt that it was through becoming engaged that I too had become a person in this place. It was in sharing the experiences of others that I had found a foothold for myself, and so a country I had at first found alien became the place I would one day call home.

A sheltered life

Reminiscing about my early life I recognise myself in the child and the young woman I was, and I realise how formative were the places in which I lived and the things I did; but sometimes I am equally surprised to discover that that was me. Was that really my life?

I see myself talking to the verger of St Peter's in the East. He is beaming with pleasure. "What a marvellous sight," he says. It was the day before my wedding and the small church adjacent to St Edmund Hall in Oxford was bursting with colour. Pink and white cottage flowers filled the windowsills, while large jugs of roses at the chancel steps and on the altar scented the air. It was a far cry from the forlorn building our group of friends had entered that morning to spring clean, and perhaps the old verger was reminded of the church in its heyday, when it was attended by dons and their families and had an organist and priest of its own. I could hardly believe that it was dressed for me and that I would be the bride walking the newly swept red carpet the next day. Malvern and I had had to put off this event for a year, but here it was, a wedding in Oxford in mid-summer 1963. It was a scene straight out of my romantic imagination and the culmination of an idyllic period of my life.

A university town is a lovely place in which to be young, surrounded by others who share a sense of life stretching out in front of them. I lived in a flat in a converted North Oxford house with three other girls. We had all finished our studies and were now taking our first steps together into the working world. Our "Crammers Club" enjoyed a whirling social life, cramming in as much as we could. Oxford Colleges were not yet co-educational and we were in great demand by the men students for their rounds of parties and balls. We were taken punting along the Isis where we picnicked under the willows. We fed ducks as they trailed alongside the boats, and after yet another College ball we would kick our shoes off throbbing feet and trail our hands in the water. We cycled everywhere, sometimes far into the Oxford countryside. It seemed always to be early summer, trees laden with blossoms and hedgerows full of Queen Anne's Lace. At weekends we bought packets of horrid-tasting reconstituted potato to bulk up the meals we cooked for the rugby players and oarsmen who came to party. In the end most of us married someone we'd met in Oxford.

Summing up the Zeitgeist, Prime Minister Harold Macmillan said, "You have never had it so good." And, as I threw up the sash windows of our flat in the mornings I would wholeheartedly agree. I felt imbued with a confidence I had not experienced before and have rarely had since.

I worked as a medical social worker at the Radcliffe infirmary, where I was part of a team of 15 white-coated social workers known quaintly as lady almoners. Our work ethos was highly professional and we were expected to have more than a smattering of medical knowledge. The units I worked on were challenging, with patients often suffering from brain tumours or head injuries, but there was always a team behind me, and many professionals to consult.

Elizabeth Turner, the head almoner, was a punctilious, pint-sized woman with a sharp mind. Nothing escaped her gimlet eye. She was often infuriated by my loquacious prose in the patients' histories or my flustered responses during ward rounds. I was a blusher, a weakness mischievously exploited by the young doctors. From among the dozen or more people participating in a round, a doctor would pick on me to answer a question then watch with glee as I helplessly felt the blush spread from neck to cheeks. Elizabeth's shrewd advice cured me. "Stop thinking about yourself, Rosemary. Concentrate on the patient and think about the information you need to convey." Her demands were exacting but her influence remained with me always. It was a wonderful training in a professional atmosphere that, years later, I would sorely miss.

One of my most difficult patients made an uncanny appearance on my wedding day. As my father and I left the flat in a chauffeur-driven car, I glimpsed him standing at a bus stop, a forlorn figure whose head injury had dislocated his personality and made him a stranger to his family and himself. His father-in-law was a peer and I had been receiving difficult phone calls from him regarding the patient's rehabilitation. There he stood, as though to remind me that when this joyous day was over, my situation may have changed but his, and others', would not have.

I was glad that he didn't see me, and with my father at my side I felt secure and buoyant. It was a quintessentially English summer's day, a few puffy white clouds in a blue sky. In New College Lane a group of American tourists clapped and called out, "Cheers to the bride!" My father looked handsome in his hired suit, his top hat on his lap. Small and balding, he had a face like Mr Pickwick's in the Dickens novel he'd read to me as a child. And though he was not much given to enthusiastic emotion, I knew that he felt happy and proud. Acquiring an academic son-in-law was a bonus.

"NPTD?" he quipped, and we laughed together.

"NPTD" was an ominous instruction often scrawled in my father's untidy hand on the calendar that hung above the coal burning stove in the kitchen of my childhood home. "No Play Today!" it commanded, as punishment for homework poorly done or a bad school report.

I was the only child of middle-class parents, cushioned, comfortable and secure. My father had a degree in History and a Masters in Education and worked for the Department of Education, first in Lancashire and later in Cornwall. He read widely and having won his own way with scholarships, revered all things academic. His father had been an erudite North-Country liberal. I never knew my grandfather Mitchell, but many of the weighty tomes on my father's shelves had come from his library. He had not had the opportunity of a university education himself, and his business had faltered badly in the depression. After the early death of his first wife, my father and his sister Miriam were raised by an unsympathetic stepmother. My father found it difficult to study at home and his clever sister was not allowed to go to university at all. She prospered in spite of her stepmother, becoming the editor of a journal in the textile industry and marrying an eminent scientist. They had no children but were vigorous walkers, played bridge and did crossword puzzles. I loved their vitality.

My mother, by contrast, was neither vigorous nor academic. Her parents were country people, simple and kind with no pretensions at all. Grandmother Mottershead had the sort of figure every small child loves to draw: round face, round body, hair in a white bun and apple cheeks radiating an all-encompassing love. My mother was described as delicate. Tall and willowy with dark hair and blue eyes, she had had enormous difficulty conceiving. She endured several miscarriages, including one of a baby girl who had gone full term. My birth must have been very special, and yet I sometimes felt excluded from the closeness of my parents' relationship. They were a little older than most of my friends' parents and were anxious not to spoil me, but I think they would have appreciated a more conventional daughter. I wanted to be out of the house having adventures, playing at being a heroine. Listening to Lady Baden-Powell on the radio one day I was fired up to become a Girl Guide, picturing myself saving victims from burning buildings, my sleeve covered in proficiency badges. I did have a very happy time in the Guides, with adventurous camps in far-flung places, but alas no heroic deeds.

On the one hand I lived a protected existence doing all the typical middle-class things like riding, ballet and Guides, but on the other I was allowed to travel alone by train to school, and in the holidays I was free to roam for miles with a gaggle of friends in the sand hills bordering our house. Often we were out for most of the day, returning only for meals and bed. I found it difficult to sit still and above all I loved to talk. At my happy little prep school I earned more black beetles for disruptive behaviour than red stars for good. It was the era of dip pens and inkwells and I always managed to let a blob of ink escape which I then inevitably smudged on the page. My elegant mother was exasperated by my clumsiness. When my teacher told her that I wrote like a chimney sweep, the letters "NPTD" appeared on the calendar and I was given pages from Anna Sewell's *Black Beauty* to sit and copy out. How I hated that horse!

When the usual shadows of adolescence began to creep into my blissful existence, they were compounded by my disappointing scholastic performance. This was something of a surprise to everyone because, although I was no good at arithmetic, I was an articulate child who devoured books. My father had read the Brontës and Austen to me while my friends were still on Enid Blyton. I had always been allowed to join in adult conversation and was considered somewhat quaint and precocious. I loved talking with my friends' mothers or with a childless couple who lived on our road, and enjoyed conversing with my father's colleagues when they came to dinner. My parents were keen for me to attend Merchant Taylors, the school where most of my friends would be going, so I sat their 11 Plus entrance exam as well as the one for the local high school. When I failed both, my father summoned me to his study.

The room smelt of ink and Three Nuns tobacco. Several large official envelopes, some still closed with sealing wax, lay on the roll-top desk. In a glass-fronted pear wood bookcase were the leather-bound encyclopaedias in which I loved to pore over the etchings of my heroines, from Joan of Arc to World War One nurse and spy, Edith Cavell. My father looked at me over the top of his spectacles as I came in, long-legged and awkward.

"Well, Rosemary," he sighed, "what are we going to do?"

I felt the sting of not being good enough when my friends had all made the grade, but I was determined to put on a brave face. I suspected that my maths marks had obliterated my prospects, but I also knew that the high school had been rather impressed with my command of English and had asked for an interview. So to the interview I went and I got into the school. But from the outset I was a fish out of water. The children around me were rougher, their houses smaller, their accents stronger. Suddenly it was clear just how middle class my life and mores were. Single-parent families had been exotic in the novels I'd read; fathers who deserted their children had presented intriguing mysteries. But in real life these situations appalled me. All my snobbish traits rose to the surface and I was unable to sense my adventure in such an alien place. My robust spirit deserted me and I was very unhappy.

My parents removed me and I was sent instead to Trinity Hall, a Methodist private school where I stayed on as a boarder when eventually, they moved to Cornwall. I loved it and soon made friendships that have lasted for life. Maths remained a stumbling block but an English teacher from Dublin with flaming red hair and a rapier wit brought Shaw's *St Joan* to life as well as a string of Irish poets. We nicknamed her Peony after the red flowers in the school garden. Town was forbidden but its allure irresistible, and bunking out always involved climbing out of dormitory windows. Years later when I described these adventures to my own daughters they hooted with incredulous laughter. "It sounds just like St Trinian's!" The boarding school students in the book and films of the same name were infamous for their flaunting of the rules.

Boys, of course, were a forbidden species and when I encountered them later at university, life took a very exciting turn. My first year as a student in English and History at Birmingham passed in a haze of parties, dances, conversations and fun, and before long, failure loomed once more. Again I found myself facing my father.

"And now what, Rosemary?" he asked.

Different study, different house, but the same ambience, with the smell of his tobacco and the sting of my shortcoming. We sat down at a dark oak table laden with his files and reports, the same one on which my father had had his appendix taken out as a small boy, and confronted the question.

I had shown some early interest in social work, after an almoner had come to speak to us at school, but I'd not been encouraged in this. "Can't you think of something *nicer*, my dear?" my grandmother had asked, speaking for the whole family. When my father and I emerged from his study this time, it was to tell my mother that I would pursue training in medical social work. In compliance with social work theory at the time, I would have to work for a year in a menial job. My father would arrange for lodgings and a position at Dingles department store in Plymouth, just across the border in Devon.

My mother crumpled. "A shop. Oh dear," she said.

It was a year of hard, physical work that opened my eyes to the drudgery of many people's lives and offered a taste of the antagonism that can exist between boss and employee. I began to take more seriously what went on in the world around me and during the next few years at Bristol University I continued to develop this interest. As well as enjoying all the usual student fun I was also secretary of the United Nations Society, voted for the Liberal Party and expressed vehement opposition to apartheid.

During the university holidays I worked with the archaically titled Association for Distressed Gentlefolk, administering grants to people who had fallen on hard times. My brief experience in a state high school had given me glimpses of a socio-economic reality very different from my own, and from the house-calls I now made, it was clear to me that Harold Macmillan's cheerful description of the times did not apply to everyone. I saw people living in the most meagre of circumstances. I visited a professor of English from the University of Cairo who had lost his job after the Suez crisis and now lived in a one-roomed apartment with his wife; a musician whose illness had demoted him from the position of first violin in a major English orchestra to an alcove under the arches near one of London's stations; a colonel's widow living in a single room in a London house where she played bridge with her neighbours on top of an orange box, her gracious manner disguising an alcohol addiction. Despite their reduced circumstances, many of these people demonstrated a resilience that I admired.

At last, after a year at the Almoners' Institute in London, I found myself in my first job at the Radcliffe in Oxford, a job and place that I loved. There followed the happiest of times, during which I worked and played in equal measure. Life was sometimes giddy with fun, but we were all becoming much more engaged with serious issues and I would soon come face to face with a challenging one of my own.

"I've met the man you're going to marry!" declared my flatmate Patsy Tranfield one late afternoon outside the squash courts where we had gone for a game. A student at the London School of Economics, her chutzpah never failed to impress me. "He's a Rhodes Scholar…," she said.

I flourished my squash racquet. "Well, where is he then?" I asked cheekily.

"…and a South African."

"Forget it," I shot back. "Never a South African." I ended the conversation and concentrated on the game ahead.

Patsy bided her time. She was engaged to be married that summer to a student at St Edmund Hall where she sang in the choir, and it was there that she had spied the South African. Attracted by his looks she had fallen into conversation with him, and finding that his interests coincided with mine, she decided to match-make. She disapproved of the boyfriend I was seeing at the time and was determined that all her friends should be as happily engaged as she was.

Curiosity overcame me and I started attending the choir rehearsals with her. Before long I was in conversation with the handsome South African too. I had met English-speaking South Africans before but never an Afrikaner. Malvern's mother was Afrikaans and his parents were card-carrying members of the Nationalist Party and faithful members of the Dutch Reformed Church. As the son of a railway stationmaster, he had grown up simply. There was no silver spoon in his mouth.

Getting to know him was exciting. He had come to Oxford to read English literature and was curious about the world in a refreshing way, looking with wonder at all things English and keen to explore the places he had previously only read about in books. In his years as a student in South Africa he had developed strong anti-apartheid views, but he was adamant about one thing: he would be going back to his country.

I found a shelf of books about South Africa in the Oxford public library and started reading. My simplistic condemnation of all things South African grew more nuanced as I read, and discussions with Malvern helped me to glimpse some of the complexities involved. As our friendship developed I became convinced that Patsy had matched us perfectly. He, on the other hand, secretly doubted that I would be able to make my life in his country, and in years to come I would look back with astonishment at how little I understood and how ill-prepared I was for life in one of the most complex societies on earth.

We became engaged during a blissful weekend in Paris and planned to marry shortly after Malvern's final exams. He and my mother got on well and my father enjoyed debating with him. It must have been hard for them, knowing that their only daughter was going to live in a distant and troubled country, but never did they make me feel guilty.

I felt deep gratitude to my father as he sat beside me in the car carrying us to St Peter's on my wedding day. I also felt grateful knowing how close his relationship with my mother was. It gave me confidence as I prepared to take this enormous step away from them.

My father's strength was doubly important because he knew the anxieties and concerns Malvern and I had shared up to this point. We were to have been married a year earlier.

Arrangements had begun but were fortunately far from completed when one weekend Malvern disappeared. He lived in a house with three others and none of them knew where he was. I was stunned and at a complete loss. His friends were helpful and my flatmates tried to console me, but I found it impossible to be passive or patient. In my distress I turned to a South African couple with whom Malvern and I had become friends.

Alex and Jenny Boraine had voyaged to England on the same Union Castle boat as Malvern had three years earlier. Alex had studied theology at Oxford and later would become President of the Methodist Church of Southern Africa and deputy chairperson of the TRC. Right now though, they were in Windsor Great Park acting as wardens in an international hostel. It was there that I phoned them. My mother asked me later why I had chosen to go to them when I had so many English friends – and I think she emphasised the word "English" – who would have helped me. I don't think I had any expectation that Malvern would be there, but suspecting the worries he had about taking me home with him, I felt that talking to older and wiser South Africans might help me grasp the situation.

The Green Line bus to Windsor gave my muddled thoughts time to sort themselves into a list of basic certainties. I knew that Malvern loved me. I knew that our lives belonged together. I knew that we shared enough to make our marriage possible. And I felt sure that his present panic was simply the result of the combined pressures of his final exams and the wedding preparations. I discussed these things with the Boraines. They were sympathetic and shared my relief when Malvern eventually turned up. It transpired that he had taken a bus to Stratford, where he had walked the streets, wandered by the river and sat in the Cobweb café, trying to sort out all the anxieties besetting him. When he finally contacted his housemates, they urged him to make his way immediately to Windsor.

Windsor Great Park is vast. The castle occupies just a small part of it. Among the ancient trees, green with summer leaves, swathes of mown grass formed miles of broad track for riders. Malvern and I tramped these pathways, this way and that, the entire day, talking, explaining, apologising, trying to understand, to find a way forward.

"Why did you leave? What are you afraid of? Can it be that bad?"

"You don't understand. I can't take you home. I can barely go home myself."

It dawned on me that Malvern's anxiety was not just about taking me to South Africa. It was about his own return to a beloved homeland that had become in many ways alien to him. He had become a different person in Oxford. How would he fit in again? The only conversations he'd had with family and friends for the past three years had been conducted over muffled phone lines that made people sound as if they were speaking from under the ocean. He and his past life existed in different realities.

When we had told each other all our fears, yet felt certain that we still wanted to be together, we agreed to postpone the wedding for a year. Malvern would teach at Whitney Grammar School while I continued to work at the Radcliffe.

When the car pulled up at St Peter's church, the red carpet lay stretched from aisle to pavement and my bridesmaids, headed up by my great friend Caroline Starling, awaited me. Caroline and I had met at Bristol University and trained to become almoners together, and though our lives would be lived on different continents, we would always count one another as sisters.

The window boxes in the St Edmund Hall quad were ablaze with scarlet geraniums, the champagne flowed freely and there were strawberries in abundance. My mother, always well dressed, outdid herself that day in a pink petal hat chosen to contrast with the navy of her dress and coat. She and my father, as they moved among the guests, were truly happy and

I felt pleased to have brought them some pleasure at last. Years later, after their deaths, my confidence in their close relationship was confirmed when I found their love letters and was moved by the depth of emotion expressed in them.

There followed an idyllic rural year in Elsfield, a village famous for its view of the Oxford spires and once home to John Buchan, a Scottish novelist who was once a government administrator in post-Boer War South Africa. Having read the Buchan adventure novels while still at school, I now reread them in Elsfield, absorbing the African connections and thinking about the author going to South Africa in 1901. The rector of the attractive Elsfield church had spent much of his life as a missionary in Africa, and Malvern and I enjoyed chatting with him and listening to his reminiscences. It was as though Africa had begun to beckon. And yet it would be two more years before we reached South Africa, and by then we would be a family of four.

Not a person

"I'm sorry, Sir, your wife is not a person in this country."

An officious customs operative had my blue embossed British passport in his hand. His thick South African accent was incomprehensible to me. We were in the customs shed at the Port Elizabeth docks, waiting for our car to be unloaded. Malvern did what he could to push the proceedings on, while Matthew ran his toy car along a dusty shelf and Anna niggled in my arms, my milk seeping through my blouse.

It was early 1966 and we were finally in Africa after an 18-month detour to America during which Malvern had taught as an assistant professor in the department of English at the University of Kansas in Lawrence. It had been a carefree year filled with firm new friends and happy memories and in many ways it helped ease me into the unfamiliar life that was to come.

Our first Christmas in the US was spent in Oklahoma with Don and Betsy Bell who took us to their family home in Muskogee where no fewer than three Christmas trees lit up the house. It was my first festive season away from my parents, with whom Christmas had always been a discreet, low-key affair. Here the occasion was rambunctious, overindulgent and altogether delightful, passing in a glow of gourmet eating and a surfeit of brandy Alexanders.

I worked one morning a week at a nursery school for disadvantaged children and saw for the first time the socio-economic realities some black people faced. In spite of their welfare cheques, they seemed sunk in a miasma of poverty, the mothers often victims of abuse from unemployed and frustrated husbands. These scenes began to introduce me to the gross contrasts I would find in South Africa.

The prospect of pursuing an academic life in the United States was attractive, though Malvern would have had to study immediately for his PhD. My chances of being the breadwinner were slim as my qualifications would have had to be reviewed and I was pregnant with Anna. In the end though, Malvern's strong feeling that he should return to South Africa prevailed. We had made friends with a South African couple in Lawrence who were graduates of Rhodes University. Ian Macdonald was a philosophy student at the University of Kansas and Gus was working as a char. When Malvern spotted an advertisement for a job in the English department at Rhodes they urged him to apply for it and, sight unseen, it was his.

Ian's and Gus's enthusiasm had heartened me as I prepared for my life in a foreign land, but driving from Port Elizabeth to Grahamstown through low hills, thorn bushes, aloes and gashes of ochre soil where the road had been laid, the customs official's words echoed in my head. No, this was *not* my country. And it was clear that it would indeed take a long time for me to become a person here.

Malvern quickly began to settle and make his name in the small university community, while I felt like an appendage, defined by his identity and dependent on his status. Sometimes it seemed to me that everyone was related or had known each other in previous lives. The network of relationships and shared histories spread like webs over the parochial society, excluding the newcomer. No-one knew my history; no-one shared my memories. Like the early settlers of this town, I was assailed by homesickness.

Grahamstown was founded by British settlers who came in a wave of immigration in the 1800s. In Britain, the Napoleonic wars and the agrarian and industrial revolutions had led to massive unemployment, and people were attracted by promises of land in Africa and new beginnings for themselves and their families. At the same time these settlers were pawns in a colonial conflict. Grahamstown was a military outpost on the extreme eastern frontier of the Cape Colony, where a settled white population was strategically desirable as a buffer against the displaced indigenous peoples being held at bay across the Fish River.

The voyage by ship must have been extremely arduous. The boats were buffeted unbearably in rough seas, and in the crowded conditions onboard, sickness was common. Measles and smallpox accounted for many deaths. When the voyagers finally arrived at Algoa Bay the view was dismal. They had to wade to the shore, and where Port Elizabeth now lies there was no town to welcome them, just a small fort, a few houses and huts, and many tents. The Reverend William Shaw, the minister who arrived from England in 1821 and played an important role in the early days of the Methodist church in the Eastern Cape, wrote of his landing, "Separated by six thousand miles of ocean from all you were wont to love and enjoy in your native country, ... the hearts of many sank within them and the inquiry was often reiterated, 'Can this be the fine country, the land of promise to which we have been allured by highly coloured descriptions, and by pictures drawn in our imaginations?' We are deceived and ruined, was the hasty conclusion of many." How they must have wished to return home. Whenever we visited Port Elizabeth in those early days and I saw a Union-Castle liner docked in the bay, I too wished I could escape.

As I began to explore Grahamstown's cultural museums and saw the fine furniture and *objets d'art* the settlers had brought with them, I wondered at their expectations and marvelled at their courage and tenacity. Trying to establish themselves in this alien land, they had to confront droughts, unproductive soil and deadly conflicts with the Xhosa people. How often they must have yearned for the more accommodating land they had left behind. In the cathedral I came upon plaques in memory of these pioneers, with epitaphs like, "Treacherously killed by the kaffirs." Such words revealed not only the alienation between the peoples involved in the conflict but also – and more tellingly for me at that stage – the dreadful shocks the settlers faced.

Nevertheless, although I found myself empathising with these people, it seemed strange and unacceptable to me that they were still held in such veneration in the Eastern Cape.

The 1820 settlers and their descendants seemed to be regarded as nothing less than aristocracy in the rather inward-looking white society of Grahamstown. While I could identify with their plight, something in me balked at their undeniable story of colonial dominance and oppression. It was just one of many moral dilemmas I would have to confront in my new life.

Like most South African towns, the Grahamstown I got to know in the late sixties was divided into three racially distinct parts. Fairly prosperous looking white residential areas surrounded the central business district, a smaller section for coloureds clustered just beyond the railway line, and beyond that lay the large African residential area. Unlike most South African towns, however, Grahamstown contained all its distinct racial communities within a single bowl surrounded by hills. In fact, the townships were visible from our front door. By day we could see Tantyi, Fingo Village and Makana's Kop (or Joza) sprawling up the hill to the east, and at night we could hear the hubbub of crowded community life.

We were not in what was considered one of the prime areas of white Grahamstown, and definitely on the "wrong" side of the tracks. A good deal of township traffic passed our door, with spans of oxen pulling wagonloads of firewood and donkeys trotting by trailing carts. When we decided to buy here, more than once we were asked, "But who will your children play with?"

We were attracted to the house in Market Street for its spaciousness. We could picture it whitewashed, with slate roof and simple lines, reminiscent of a Derbyshire farmhouse. On a lecturer's salary it was also all we could afford. Other more modern houses we had seen at the lower end of the market were poky and boring by comparison. But this one was in a bad state of neglect. When we first entered, our legs were covered instantly in a swarming mass of fleas. I was shocked as I associated them with slums and filth. I had no idea that they were a common hazard in the Eastern Cape, especially in old buildings.

The house was divided into three flats with hardboard partitions, and was further spoiled by an ugly balcony out front and a tin-roofed lean-to at the back. The big garden was a mass of weeds, broken bricks and the ruins of hen houses and pigeon lofts. Malvern had more vision than I did and was enthusiastic from the start, knowing that the house was full of promise. So we bought it and began the long adventure of making it our own.

In many ways Grahamstown seemed like a small English market town straight out of a novel. The streets were wide with little traffic and the High Street had a particularly colonial air. At one end stood the Herbert Baker buildings of Rhodes University with their broad steps and tower, and at the opposite end, Gilbert Scott's cathedral spire stretched into the sky. In between were houses with cool verandas, bustling shops, a magistrate's court and a Supreme Court. One of the hotels had red carpets, palms in large tubs and waiters wearing white gloves and fezzes. One would not have been surprised to see the author Rudyard Kipling or British army officer General Gordon of Khartoum striding out. Both had in fact visited Grahamstown and Gordon had taken tea in the drawing room of the very house we had just bought.

The Church Square was dominated on one side by the Anglican cathedral and on the other by a rather fine 19th century Methodist church, where an avenging angel, looking as though she might at any moment soar heavenward, commemorated the Boer War. The Standard Bank with its neo-classical columns lent an air of the British Raj. Various shops with splendid, picturesque facades faced onto the square. There was a bookshop with panes of coloured Victorian glass in its doors and windows, and glass-fronted bookcases within. Stepping inside, I felt as though I had entered the pages of a Dickens novel. The proprietor served me with deference and old-world courtesy, his black coat shiny at the elbows and his suit in need of a trip to the dry cleaners. I imagined him sitting on a high stool dipping his quill into an inkwell and writing in a leather-bound ledger. The ambience of outdated gentility did not give the impression of a thriving commercial business. Years later, when our son took a holiday job there, the then proprietor would be astonished by Matthew's sales patter.

"How is it that every customer seems to be your friend?" he would ask.

"They're not, Sir," was Matthew's cheeky reply, "but this is the way to sell books."

The local newspaper, *Grocott's Mail*, was produced from the back of this shop. It had been family-run for a hundred years and beneath its front-page banner it carried the boast, "South Africa's oldest family newspaper. Established 1870. Liberty and Progress." It seemed at times to be stuck in the 19th century. A journalist friend of ours said that when he was working on Bloemfontein's local newspaper in the 1950s, copies of *Grocott's Mail* would arrive still addressed to The Editor, *The Friend*, Bloemfontein, Orange River Colony.

Opposite the square lay the equally old-fashioned Birch's Gentlemen's Outfitters and General Drapery selling school uniforms, church vestments and graduation gowns. I was astonished when I paid for my first purchase there to see my money conveyed to the cashier on overhead wires by a quaint metal shuttle. More astonishing still is that Birch's continued to use this system well into the 1990s.

I quickly learnt that if there was anything at all that my household needed, I would find it at Woods' General Store in Bathurst Street, owned and run by the Woods family for over a hundred years. It sold everything from knitting needles to pans, from aprons to marshmallows. The glass-fronted showcases were monuments to the past and throughout the next three decades I never witnessed any attempt to modernise. I was served on my first visit by one of the Mesdames Woods, with grey bun and horn-rimmed spectacles and a forbidding air of correctness that made me feel like a nuisance to be shopping there. When she presented the handwritten bill in her rather intimidating way, I felt embarrassed not to have the exact amount immediately to hand.

As well as feeling decidedly British, much of the architecture in Bathurst Street reminded me of Kansas. Like several other streets in Grahamstown it was wide enough to turn an ox wagon, and with its flat-fronted buildings it could easily have been a set for the western, *The Good, the Bad and the Ugly*. Years later I would see a great deal of this street, as the Black Sash advice office would be situated there, and on occasion it would indeed feel like the Wild West. One late afternoon while locking up, a Black Sash colleague and I looked up the street to see a young man running towards us, chased by a policeman brandishing a gun in each hand. A police van was supporting the chase, swerving in and out of the road while a crowd of onlookers cheered loudly. The fugitive was probably a petty thief, for we saw him toss a package over a gate just before he was caught. While he was being bundled into the van, we noticed someone else retrieve the packet. This person, probably a student, had been hanging out of a high window watching the proceedings. When he thought no-one was looking, he slipped along the parapet, jumped down, picked up the parcel and climbed back up again, disappearing into his window and drawing the curtains behind him. The fugitive's case drew no subsequent attention. His was just one of many arrests in those days, and as a theft case it would certainly have been unlikely to be brought to us at the advice office. And so we never did find out what the agile opportunist in the digs upstairs had found in that package.

Such experiences would however come later when I had, thankfully, found my niche. In the meantime it would require all my energy just to accept that this bewildering town was going to be my home. The climate was alien, the light too bright, the flowers too vivid in colour. The prolific dark purple bougainvillaea in suburban gardens unsettled me, making me feel claustrophobic, as though some unknown danger lurked in its deep shade.

The vastness of the landscape frightened me, as it had done in America. While Malvern had been awed by the Painted Desert in Arizona, revelling in its colouring, light and shade, I had felt a deep longing for the manageable scenery of Oxfordshire. Our little red brick cottage in Elsfield had perched on a hill from where we looked out on green and yellow chequered fields and small copses of trees. The hedgerows contained a many-layered world of twisted twigs and roots, small wild flowers and rambling berries. It was all so neat and pretty. Even the sand hills of my childhood now seemed cosy, with the star grass that pricked our legs and the familiar bee orchid, grass of Parnassus and evening primrose. Years later in Tuscany near San Gimignano, where a South African friend lived in exile, I remarked on the loveliness of the hedgerows there and she replied, "I long for the Port Jackson willow and the hot African sand under my feet." So deeply are the scenes and scents of our youth embedded within us.

Fortunately much of my energy in those early days was consumed by domestic concerns. When we arrived, Matthew was 18 months and Anna 3 months. They were joined three years later by Charlotte and shortly afterwards by Lucy. The children's early years were spent amidst the clutter and bustle of ongoing renovations at 24 Market Street. Structurally the house was fine but a great deal of scraping and painting needed to be done and the garden had to be rescued from dilapidation. Our parents, who visited us at the start of the restoration process, were horrified by the task. My father referred to the house as the "whited sepulchre" while my mother bluntly stated it needed people with money to buy it. Malvern's parents could not understand why we didn't opt for mod-con.

When Malvern returned briefly to Oxford to complete his BLitt, leaving me with the children, I was heartened to find new friends rallying around. With the restoration of the house, this sense of community grew as friends and colleagues arrived, rollers and paintbrushes in hand. We in turn helped others with the renovation of their crumbling homes. The poet Don Maclennan and his American wife Shirley had arrived at

Rhodes at the same time as us and bought a Victorian house that also needed a lot of painting. I admired Shirley and her handsome young family and longed for my own brood to become as wise and independent as hers.

During the painting process I'd do my best to keep the children out of the way, but on one occasion Matthew got into the sitting room where Malvern and fellow lecturer, André de Villiers were in the midst of a delicate wallpapering task. Matthew climbed up on the couch to watch them as they battled to get the pattern straight. Fuelled by a few beers and a discussion, no doubt on the Romantics, the job was going smoothly until Matthew started to wriggle and the hood of the grandfather clock, propped up next to him on the couch, slipped and crashed. Shards of glass and tiny splinters of wood spilled across the floor. It was heartbreaking. The 18th century walnut clock, with its delicately painted face, had stood in the hall of my grandmother's house in Cheshire. On either side, had hung portraits of Lord and Lady Vernon, for whom my grandfather had worked. And as a little girl I had gone to sleep listening to its ticks and chimes echoing in my grandmother's hallway. Now it seemed ruined.

Many items of antique furniture in our house were ingrained with stories and memories from my early life, and having them near helped me recreate the distant home that I still missed. Malvern understood this. He picked up every splinter of the shattered hood with stamp tweezers and put them all in a box. One of his mature students at the time was a skilled woodworker and craftsman, and over a few months this amazing man patiently and lovingly restored the piece. When the clock was moved back into its place in the renovated living room, flaws in the wallpapering were easier to detect than mends or joins in the walnut hood.

Steadily our lovely house emerged. In the 1860s it had been home to Bishop Nathaniel Merriman, father of John X Merriman who became Prime Minister of the Cape. The original building was completed in 1830, with a second section added when the schoolmaster Charles Grubb lived there, to house the first school in town. We found fascinating relics during the restoration. The lock on the front door, when polished up, was found to bear the crest of William IV. Lost behind the mantelpiece in the drawing room there was a daintily framed picture, embossed on plaster, of a girl holding a cat. Had it belonged to one of the Merriman daughters? Was it perhaps a kind of Christmas card that had dropped from display? In the garden we dug up old apothecary bottles and pieces of blue and white china. A letter written by Mrs Merriman records the visit of General Gordon of Khartoum. "About ten, as father and I were huddled across my Davenport, the door opened and in came Mr Huntley with General Gordon so to speak in his hand … [he] met us quite as old friends and at once launched forth into a stream of talk." We were thrilled with all this history in our living room.

Years later historians would suggest that bishop Merriman's groom, Goliath, who had lived in a hut in the garden, was none other than Mhlakaza, the uncle of the prophetess Nongqawuse. For years Goliath travelled and preached with Merriman in the remote parts of the diocese. They would read to each other from their English and isiXhosa Bibles, comparing the interpretations of scripture. He left Merriman's service, perhaps with some disenchantment, returning to his tribal home across the Kei River where, it is believed, he resumed his traditional name and customs and began preaching his own version of the gospel. In 1857, when his young niece claimed that the spirits of the ancestors had appeared to her, it was he who interpreted her visions to the people. The ancestors instructed Nongqawuse to tell the people to kill their cattle and destroy their crops, after which the dead would arise and chase the white oppressors into the sea. Mhlakaza's precise role is disputed, but he undoubtedly contributed to the debacle that led to the subsequent cattle killing and the tragic decimation of the Xhosa people.

Most often, the Eastern Cape weather was hot, dry and dusty, with veld fires filling the wind with smoke. I wondered if I would ever get over the strangeness and alienation, the hostility with which I viewed so many things. Then, stepping out of my back door into a pale green light one late afternoon, I saw flocks of birds circling against the rugged hillside behind our house. "It's not as good as the slow twilight of a long summer's evening," I thought, "but it is beautiful."

Years later we were driving to the wedding of a young friend in Port Alfred. Along the roadside the summer grasses had a pinkish tinge in the sun and the fences were smothered in blue plumbago. At one point, where the hills roll away from the road towards the sea, there was a vista of never-ending space. I was thrilled by the beauty and solace of all that space. "I love the bush and the light," I said, looking across at Malvern – and found myself completely surprised by the simultaneous thought, "I love this land."

Establishing an identity

Market Street has always been at the centre of a lot of activity. Across the road from our front door lay the square where wagonloads of merchandise were traded in the 19th century: horns, skins, pelts, feathers, pots, bracelets, beads – and piles of ivory. Once Grahamstown ceased to be a commercial hub the market traded mainly in local agricultural produce. In our early years in the town we bought fresh vegetables from the run-down sheds on the square, but as the decades passed we watched in dismay as supermarkets and fast food outlets began to arrive on our doorstep.

In typical settler style, our house fronted directly onto the street. Later suburban trends would set houses behind hedges and gates, making them less accessible to the passing traffic, but in the older parts of town there were constant knocks on doors as people from the townships walked from house to house seeking work. During my childhood in England the only strangers who had banged on the door were the occasional gypsy in a long skirt, often with a baby in her arms, selling pegs or white heather, or more likely, a salesman selling small sweeping brushes from a neat little suitcase.

A frequent caller in Market Street was a man by the name of Milton. Sporting a black beret and speaking an old fashioned but articulate English, he always seemed to me to be just popping by on his way to the Reading Room at the British Museum. Although his mind had known better days, his social and political comments could be very sharp. Word was that he had been an early member of the South African Liberal Party, which had long since been banned. Knowing that Malvern was associated with the Progressive Party (he'd joined in 1959 before leaving for Oxford), Milton enjoyed baiting us on certain flaws in the opposition's manifesto. Was it not discriminatory, he taunted, to advocate a qualified franchise based on minimum levels of education and income?

Of course, he also knew precisely how to win a girl's heart and invariably I would end up putting my hand in my pocket. One day he reassured me that he had not come for money but to find out what the German word for 'lemon' was. I later discovered that he had helped himself to a sack-full from our friend's tree and was bartering with our German neighbours! I was sorry when Milton died before the new South Africa had begun to dawn.

I soon learnt that giving beggars food or money created untenable dependencies and I realised that it solved few problems. But there was no getting away from the relentless stream of need. I had encountered poverty in England and had seen the effects of social inequality in my work there, but I had not been prepared for this vast gulf between rich and poor. By comparison to those coming to our door, even we seemed rich. We had no jobs for them and not much spare money, and yet our material circumstances were worlds better than theirs. With each knock I became more oppressed by helplessness and guilt. I felt compelled to seek some sort of action. But how did I fit in and what was I to do? I had begun helping out as a volunteer at the Black Sash advice office on Saturday mornings, but I thought that if I took a job – any job at this stage – I could perhaps find ways of alleviating some of the problems on our doorstep.

One of the few Afrikaners at Rhodes at this time was the sociologist HW van der Merwe. He was known by his Afrikaans initials, "HW", which to English ears like mine sounded like "Harvey". He was probably responsible for introducing Malvern to anti-apartheid ideas as a young man. The Contact Study Group at Stellenbosch University, founded under HW's influence, had helped to shape the political thought of young Afrikaners such as Malvern and Frederik van Zyl Slabbert, who would one day become the leader of the official opposition, the

Progressive Federal Party. One of the stereotypes of the time was that all Afrikaners were nationalists and that English South Africans were generally more liberal. But I was surprised to discover in time that my fellow English-speakers were often very conservative. Many were overtly racist, while some Afrikaners were much more liberal than I was. This was indeed proving a strange society.

HW came to my rescue. He was studying white elites in South Africa and offered me a part-time job as a research assistant administering a questionnaire door-to-door. What an opportunity, not just to *do* something, but also to get a glimpse of the people behind the doors of suburban Grahamstown. Barking dogs would often bar my way and although it was not yet the era of security gates and blade wire, one house I visited did sport a hand-painted sign declaring, "This house is protected by a shotgun." Chilling messages aside, I was surprised at how many people invited me in and were willing to answer my questions. In England, where I had visited patients at their homes, I had found people much more private than these South Africans were proving.

From the poorest to the wealthiest home, the person who responded to my knock at the door was often a uniformed maid referred to as "the girl". In Kipling-esque style, she referred to her employers as "madam" or "master". In many instances she lived in, and was not the only domestic help. The smartest homes gleamed with a lustre that suggested entire teams were on hand – what a friend referred to as "servants running hot and cold". Later, in my advice office work, I would gain a very different perspective on the lives of these smiling maids who ushered me in for the interviews. Beneath the surface of most domestic arrangements there was a reality of exploitation that I was not yet able to discern.

My research formed a very small part of HW's work, but through it I learnt a great deal. I began to perceive the divisions between town and gown. For example I realised that membership of the Anglican cathedral gave one a certain patrician status; and I discerned that the legal fraternity saw themselves as a powerful elite. In all, I encountered some very colonial mentalities.

After working for HW I took a part-time job with a welfare scheme at the university, which began to give me some insight into the "other" side of Grahamstown. Some members of the white academic staff donated money each month that was made available for loans and bursaries for black service staff. My job was to assess the needs of applicants and manage the distribution of the money from a dark, poky office on campus. Always awaiting me at the door would be queues of cleaners and gardeners, each with an insoluble problem arising from the poverty trap that ensnared them all. My power to grant or withhold money, and the corresponding powerlessness of the applicants, made me feel like the feudal dispenser of old-world charity to the "deserving poor".

I often felt that I was floundering. Not only was I overwhelmed by the extent of people's need but I was also ignorant of their language and culture and aghast at their circumstances. Unemployment was rife and wages appalling. Education was not free, and school fees, books and uniforms presented extra expenses. People got themselves into debt through hire-purchase, often to have their goods repossessed when their payments lapsed. It was a job with no end. Clearly the university needed to start a proper personnel department, and this did eventually happen, though long after I had moved on.

Interestingly, the nature of the work I did, and the association it gave me with black people, did not make me popular in some circles. One right-wing professor who was also a warden at one of the halls of residence described me, along with the then professor of anthropology and a woman who had started a feeding scheme for children, as the three most dangerous people in Grahamstown. This was rather startling. At that time I was not prominently involved in any political activity and was comparatively unknown – unlike my fellow accused. Perhaps I was achieving some identity after all.

Being young and idealistic, Malvern was creating a reputation of his own within the Progressive Party. In 1970 he was chosen as the party's parliamentary candidate for the Albany region and there followed a few months of intense party-political energy in our home.

We'd witnessed elections American-style when, living in Kansas we'd heard Hubert Humphrey speak at a razzmatazz event when he was running for the vice-presidency. There, politics seemed lightweight and glitzy. In South Africa, by contrast, elections were fought over deadly serious and deeply moral issues. The first post-war election of 1948 had astounded the world by giving DF Malan's Nationalist Party the victory over respected international statesman and Prime Minister of the Union of South Africa, Jan Smuts. Malan had seemed bad enough, but far harsher Afrikaner nationalists were to succeed him.

The official opposition, led by Sir de Villiers Graaff, seemed merely to promote apartheid with a kinder face. In fact, the United Party seemed anachronistic to me. Many of its members harked back to a bygone age. The MPs I met with their cravats and moustaches all spoke in clipped tones, mostly about World War II.

With the demise of the Liberal Party, the Progressives, born in a split from the UP, had become the only legal opposition worth supporting. It was not exactly radical. It did not believe in One Man, One Vote, but in a qualified franchise; a policy which seemed archaic and patronising, but for many whites at that time it was a revolutionary and dangerous idea. At least the Progressive Party was unequivocally opposed to separate development. Helen Suzman served as this party's sole representative in parliament for thirteen years, where she was vilified by MPs of other parties for the tenacity of her opposition. She was especially known for relentlessly ferreting out failures and sins with which to confront the ruling party. This indomitable woman showed a completely different side to her character when she stayed at our home. She charmed the whole family by behaving like a beloved grandmother, allowing the children to clamber all over her bed and gleefully distributing the jelly beans she had brought.

Malvern was inexperienced in politics and not greatly accomplished as a public speaker. He especially lacked the stabbing witticisms and quick repartee of most politicians, besides which he tended to be trusting of people, which would surely make him a poor politician. But he made a brave stand and I was proud of him. I supported his campaign as well as I could with three small children in tow and a fourth on the way, but one day, heavily pregnant and carrying trays of food up steep stairs to feed the party workers, I overheard someone say, "She can work as hard as she likes, but if she can't vote it's not much good." It was a slap in the face, but true.

I was still very ambivalent about identifying myself as a South African and clung to my British passport. I had already taken on so much that was alien to my Englishness that this document seemed like my last hope, my umbilical link to a country that in honesty, I still regarded as superior. I did become a permanent resident, but it was going to be a giant leap for me to become a citizen and voter.

The Progressive campaign was run from a rather seedy room in a long-ago hotel that had fallen on hard times. The curtains smelled of stale cigarette smoke and the threadbare carpet was stained. The records of the branch were kept in cardboard boxes in the wardrobe. There was no such thing as exposure on television – this marvel would only reach South Africa in 1976 – and very little on radio. The party manifesto proclaimed that a vote for Malvern was "a choice, not an echo", and one advert proclaimed, "In your heart you know he's right." Stirring stuff, but one supporter went a little too far and probably lost the party some votes when he distributed a pamphlet declaring, "If Jesus Christ were alive today he would vote for Van Wyk Smith."

We knew that Malvern had slim chance of getting into parliament, yet the Progressive Party was considered a threat. Once, while we were registering voters at a table in High Street, special branch officers were observed with their binoculars trained on the tables, no doubt noting the names of supporters. Sometimes the atmosphere in the town was distinctly hostile. People would cross the road rather than greet us and for a while we were plagued at home by anonymous phone calls. Progressive Party posters were defaced and torn down and the local undertaker refused a canvassing visit from Malvern because "it would be bad for business".

Malvern became used to addressing half-empty halls and responding to hecklers. But because the party was so small and beleaguered, a special bond grew among the supporters. Once they decided, on the inspiration of Tony Giffard, a lecturer in the new journalism department at Rhodes, to undertake a whistle stop tour by train through the constituency, to take the campaign to the people. So on a Saturday morning a group of supporters packed the Kowie Express and made the 60-kilometre journey down to the coast. "Express" was a misnomer. The chugging steam train wove its way through pineapple fields, stopping at numerous small stations better described as halts. Advance publicity had gone out to all farmers, but at every stop Malvern stepped out onto a deserted platform. No one came to hear him. Nevertheless it was a festive expedition and the supporting entourage cheered and waved placards and had their photographs taken. Malvern's professor, Guy Butler, went disguised as a pineapple farmer and at each deserted stop he pretended to heckle, "What about the pineapples, Boet?"

Although Malvern had clearance from the university vice chancellor to run for parliament, he had to take unpaid leave for six weeks. In the early hours of a wet morning, weary in my pregnant state, I stood on the balcony of the magistrate's court and watched the candidates emerge after the counting of the votes. When I saw Malvern's drawn face I knew we had lost badly. The Progressives had captured 1 002 votes while the United Party retained their seat with 5 950 and the Nationalists received 3 259. For our friends in the Progs it was devastating. Nevertheless, the next day they enveloped us in true South African kindness, arriving at the house with flowers, food and lots of sympathy.

That political blow was followed by a personal one – the deaths of both my parents. My father died of a coronary, after which my mother, who was sick with cancer, came to stay with us. I was pleased to have her close because it lessened my anxiety about her, but when her condition went into remission she insisted on going home. One of the most difficult things I have ever had to do was put my mother on a plane in Port Elizabeth, knowing that I might never see her again. My mild, gracious mother, who had already lost her beloved and protective life partner, was about to face her greatest challenge on her own. I wept to see her go and was glad of the stalwart support of a friend who had taken us to the airport. My mother died a few months later, two weeks after Lucy's birth. The whole family, including me, had chickenpox. It was a bitter trial for me, thinking of her being buried without my being there. And with no siblings to share my sorrow or memories, more than ever I felt the loneliness of being an only child.

When we returned to England in 1972 for a year's sabbatical, we had the difficult job of sorting out my parents' belongings. It was strange to be there without them, but our friends were warm and supportive. We relished the cultural wealth that surrounded us and it was such a relief not to have endless beggars at the door. I felt the strong seductive pull of English life, and when the year was over I did not want to return to South Africa. But we had invested in a house and a life there, and academic jobs were hard to come by. There was also Malvern's involvement with the Progressive Party and there was no question, really, that we would not come back. My children watched me cry copious tears as our ship left Southampton. Years later, when I asked Anna if she remembered my distress, my eldest daughter told me that as a small child she had always felt that I wanted to be somewhere else. Such an unsettling experience to have given my young children.

We'd been back for a year when Malvern's father died after a protracted illness. Fortunately his parents were not as far away as mine had been and he had a brother who shared the responsibility of caring for them. But our relationship with them was fraught. It was a situation of my making, which I later greatly regretted. They were kind and generous people but conservative Afrikaners who viewed me as something of a communist. It does me no credit that I took them head-on, criticising all that I saw wrong in their society. Already feeling alienated from their Oxford-educated son, they now had to watch him defend his wife's arguments against them. Malvern was sorely torn in these situations. I never mended the relationship with my father-in-law but did manage to make amends with my mother-in-law before she died a few years later. She loved her grandchildren and was generous in her acknowledgement of my parenting.

In 1974 Malvern was persuaded to stand again. This time it was trickier as there was no Nationalist Party candidate, making it a straight fight between the two opposition parties. The Progressives were accused of splitting the vote. This meant that a lot of energy which should have gone into attacking the government's policies was dissipated in fighting the official opposition. My own citizenship issue had become clearer in my mind by now. I was feeling much more committed to South Africa but had decided that I would not cast my vote until all citizens could do the same. Malvern supported my stance, and in every subsequent whites-only election until 1994, I was pleased to have friends who too, chose not to participate, condemning apartheid elections as morally wrong and invalid.

This time our children were able to be more involved in Malvern's campaign. Matthew was an energetic little boy of 10. On election day he stood from morning to evening on the steps of the magistrate's court, socks steadily wrinkling down around his ankles while handing out pamphlets for his father. The United Party took Albany again, with the Progressives polling 1 800 votes this time. Nationally, however, the outcome for the Progressive Party was very exciting. Helen Suzman was joined in parliament by six new Progressive MPs, including Frederik van Zyl Slabbert and Alex Boraine, both of whom we knew, admired and trusted. We were elated, but it was to be the last of Malvern's attempts to get into parliament. Three years later the United Party was unable to retain its seat. Sadly, though, it was not the Progressives who ousted them. In 1977 the Nationalists won Albany for the first time ever, to raucous celebrations. "That's the end of the Jews and Little England!" someone called out from the cavalcade of cars celebrating the victory. But four years later EK Moorcroft, a broad-shouldered giant from the Winterberg, at last won the constituency for the Progressive Party. I felt a wry bitterness when I overheard an acquaintance say, "This is the moment we have been waiting for." Ten years previously those same people had not made their mark for Malvern or the party.

With Malvern becoming more and more politically active, I was happy to be offered a new challenge of helping to run a nursery school. For the next nine years Dickory Dock was to become a large part of my life. For a short time it included Charlotte and Lucy, Matthew and Anna having started school. I had no teaching experience and scant knowledge of nursery schools, while my colleague Gill McJannet, who was English too, was a qualified teacher, played the piano and was altogether more suited to the task than I was. But I loved children and valued the cheerful nature of the work.

Pre-school education was not yet the norm but Dickory Dock met a growing need and was very popular. It occupied part of an old house with a large stoep and hedged garden. Apart from its welcoming, bright red gate it was a little scruffy around the edges and by textbook standards it stretched the rules, with too many children for just one qualified teacher. Inevitably, it was for white children only and very Euro-centric, but it was a happy place, a world of play, stories and songs, excursions to farms, harvest festivals and concerts. One little girl, when confronting the move to "real" school, said with a heavy sigh, "If only Dickory Dock went up to matric!"

I had joined the Black Sash as early as 1968 and was participating more and more in their political and human rights activities. In time the nursery school would become a daily haven from the tensions and cares that were to be my regular fare in that organisation. The Terrorism Act defined terrorism as anything from participating in the armed struggle to "embarrassing the administration of the affairs of the state". To the Black Sash, embarrassing the administration of the affairs of the state was virtually its *raison d'être*.

The organisation had arisen in 1955 on a wave of outrage regarding the Senate Bill, a Nationalist ploy to remove coloured voters from the Cape voters' roll. Six white women at a tea party set a protest in motion, and support grew rapidly until a league of 10 000 was holding marches, convoys, demonstrations and all-night vigils. The women were mostly middle class, liberal minded, white and English speaking, and they called themselves the Women's Defence of the Constitution League. But the press nicknamed them The Black Sash, after the sashes they wore over their shoulders as symbols of mourning for the death of South Africa's constitution.

The early demonstrations included "haunting" government ministers wherever they went. As an official left Jan Smuts airport in Johannesburg, a coded message would be sent to league members in the next city. An "order for carnations" in Port Elizabeth meant that a particular minister was on his way there. "Orders" for roses, proteas and a whole range of floribunda represented the movements of others. Forewarned by these messages, Sash members in all the major centres would be at the ready to welcome unsuspecting politicians at their destinations. A row of silent white women draped in black sashes must have had a peculiarly discomfiting effect. Running these gauntlets became a matter of acute embarrassment to the ministers of state and turned the Black Sash into a fiercely hated adversary.

When the battle was lost and the Senate Act was passed, the Black Sash turned its attention to the general legislation underpinning apartheid. Membership shrank from the initial flurry and enthusiasm, and for the next 40 years it continued as a very small but resilient organisation.

From the first time I heard about the Black Sash I felt drawn to its human rights agenda. But my own start in the organisation was less than illustrious. In the minutes of a meeting in 1968 I am recorded as demurring that "we as mere housewives" could hardly be expected to achieve much. I was of course howled down, and in time my courage and vision grew. I began to feel politically at home, and as I became more and more active in the organisation I was drawn into ever more challenging situations, worlds apart from the seclusion of Dickory Dock. At times these two contrasting sides of my life collided rather absurdly.

In 1974 the State President, Jim Fouché, came to Grahamstown to open the Settlers Monument – English South Africa's reply to the Voortrekker Monument in Pretoria, which honoured the achievements of the Afrikaner. The Voortrekker Monument is a place of pilgrimage but little else. By contrast, thanks mainly to the remarkable vision of Guy Butler, the Settlers Monument is a living one. It boasts a fine theatre and conference rooms and became home to the annual National Arts Festival, an event which in time became a truly South African celebration.

Perched on a hilltop, the monument dominates the town, square and grey and forbidding. Its building caused some controversy, many people feeling that the money could have been put to better use in the townships across the valley. When, in the turbulent 1980s, the army placed searchlights on the hilltop to rake those townships at night, the Settlers Monument became synonymous with the operations of the hateful police state. It took a long time for that image to be erased. The poet Tony Delius was reputed to have said of the monument that after the revolution it would make the biggest beer hall in the Eastern Cape.

There was controversy surrounding the opening to be performed by the State President, a nationalist Afrikaner, when the monument was dedicated to the British settlers and their reputedly more liberal values. On the eve of the event a small posse of protesters including some Black Sash women furtively daubed anti-apartheid slogans in red paint on the imposing southeast wall of the building, visible from the national road. But in the nursery school, spurred on, I suppose, by memories of royal visits in England, Gill and I prepared the children for the visit of the president's so-called "White Train". I phoned the railway headquarters and sent a special request that the president should wave as the train passed through the West Hill station as there would be children gathered there. We made small replicas of the South African flag and held a practice ceremony during which I huffed and chuffed like the train passing by, cheered on by the little cluster of republican flags.

The great day arrived and we went up the hill to the small station where we corralled the children with skipping ropes and waited. There were small prep school boys too, pushing and shoving on the platform. What a disappointment it was when the train with its silver insignia finally arrived. The president and his wife were dressed in very ordinary clothes, and although he did wave his top hat, it was the chef who proved far more exciting in his dazzling white uniform and puffy headgear. We regretted not having made a cardboard crown for the State President to wear. While we had much to laugh about on the day, I went home wondering what I was doing encouraging adulation of an official representative of apartheid, when I actually identified far more with those who had vilified him in red paint the night before.

One of the first big events at the new monument was the International Convention of Women held in December 1975. The purpose, besides celebrating International Women's Year, was a critical appraisal of women's participation in shaping the future of the world. It was a glittering event, with a host of diverse women who had achieved remarkable feats on a global stage, arriving in our small South African town. Many of the guests stayed in private homes. We entertained Dame Kathleen Kenyon, the archaeologist who handled the dig of biblical Jericho. She was a past director of the British School of Archaeology in Jerusalem and had been principal of St Hugh's College, Oxford. She was also no mean cricket player. Our small son was at the stage of batting balls and constructing makeshift wickets at every opportunity. He was somewhat startled to be confronted by a large Englishwoman lumbering down our lawn and bowling him out. Her voice was deep and her presence commanding. At the introductory session of the conference she sat squarely on the stage, legs wide apart, displaying her rather awesome knickers, the likes of which I had not seen since my school days.

South African women of different races and life experiences had had few opportunities to live alongside each other and engage as equals. Even anti-apartheid groups like the Black Sash were racially segregated due to divide-and-rule legislation. And though we probably came closer than any other white organisation to representing the cause of the oppressed, as individuals we gained little experience in open and equal relations with black people.

Staying together in the university residences was a new experience for many and the conference gave rise to tensions and conflicts. Many a discussion devolved into a debate along racial lines, often sidelining the international women and their contributions. Margaret Mead, the famous American anthropologist, became an ad hoc conciliator, mediating in several late night debates. She appeared at the conference in a flowing bottle-green cloak, crook in hand, like an ancient goddess from Homer. Years later we learnt that the conference had been underwritten by the controversial Department of Information, a mouthpiece for Nationalist Party propaganda. Whatever they had hoped to achieve by it, they could not have foreseen the controversies that surfaced among the South African women present.

I felt out of my depth in relating to my countrywomen during that conference, and back within the confines of the Black Sash organisation I wasn't feeling much stronger. I often felt intimidated by members such as the then chairperson, Doreen Kelly, who reminded me of my teachers and made me feel as though I was back in school. An Oxford graduate, from a time when it had been unusual and difficult for women from the colonies to go to Oxbridge, Doreen spoke in crisp, precise tones and did not suffer fools gladly. She declined the drawing rooms and bridge tables in favour of political activism, but always appeared in gloves and hat, even at a protest demonstration. Once, when our minute books and papers were seized by the Special Branch, Doreen, undaunted, bearded them in their den. In those days their activities were shrouded in secrecy but she ferreted out the exact position of their offices, found a locked door and hammered on it. Bolts were drawn back and a policeman opened up. "You have seized our records and I have come to take them back," Doreen said sharply. When a bewildered policeman protested that they had done nothing wrong, she emphatically replied, "I should hope not! You *are* the police."

Sometimes the younger Sash members were the most daunting. Sociologists, lawyers, journalists, they were of radical persuasion and mostly very knowledgeable about South African affairs. Many of them had been active in student politics. In contrast, my early forays into political activity had been muddled and naïve. In the United Nations Society at Bristol University I had been swept up on the wave of enthusiasm and zeal for global betterment without ever really becoming informed about the principles of the UN. Similarly during the Suez crisis I'd been more preoccupied with evading lonely Egyptians in exile than with the political issues at hand. Now I found myself amongst young women who were extremely well informed on the issues of the day, could think on their feet and were excellent public speakers. It was a humbling experience and an excellent education for me.

In the early years I sometimes felt that I stood out as someone who did not quite belong in radical company. I wondered what people thought when they saw me participating in protest stands. In Grahamstown these were always held around the cathedral, a prominent spot visible to all the traffic circling that busy area. Permission for each stand had to be sought from the municipality. In keeping with the established Black Sash style, we stood silently and with heads bowed, sometimes holding posters, and often we received insults and rebukes. Sometimes a car would come past with some of my nursery school children bobbing up and down in the back. Their mothers might give an encouraging wave, or might as easily look the other way.

For a while in the 1970s a unique phenomenon occurred in Grahamstown. Whenever the Black Sash held a protest stand, a lone figure would appear on the opposite corner, a large woman dressed in black and draped in a broad white sash. She was the widow of a prominent Supreme Court Judge. Sometimes she was accompanied by a child straight out of Louisa May Alcott's *Little Women*, in white dress, long white socks and a white bow. There they stood, silently staring us down, as faithful in their demonstration as we were in ours.

During the 1980s when she had gone and times had become harder, our demonstrations came to resemble hers in that only one person at a time was allowed to stand. For these demonstrations we chose the west door of the cathedral, facing the traffic coming down High Street. A support person was always out of sight behind the cathedral door, armed with a sheet of instructions, "What To Do In Case Of Arrest." When I think of standing in that doorway, I remember feeling frozen. Whether from cold or fear I wasn't always sure. It was not something I enjoyed doing. The anxiety aside, standing still and keeping silent are not things that come easily to me. My other vivid memory of that windy and highly visible spot is of a young policeman awkwardly clutching a subversive Black Sash poster emblazoned with the words "Thou Shalt Not Kill", while the Sash member fished deep in her coat pocket for the letter of permission he had asked her to produce. We doubted that many passers-by would have spotted the irony.

As the activities of the Black Sash enveloped me I began to find, if at first timidly, a voice and an identity. The organisation was destined to become an important and fulfilling focus in my life and the friendships I would make there would be close and lasting. I mourned my parents for a long time, feeling that their deaths had cut me even further adrift; but I realise that, had it not been for their relatively early deaths I might never have been able to get involved to the extent that I did. With ageing parents on another continent I may well have been flying back and forth for years, struggling to put down the roots that today are grappled into the rocky soil of the Eastern Cape.

Working days

St Clement's Anglican Church was situated in the coloured community next to the railway station. The Black Sash hired its hall for our weekly advice office sessions, setting out Sunday school benches and sometimes pews from the church for our clients to sit in while they waited. The hall was bitterly cold in winter and stifling in summer. Rain on the zinc roof sounded like pebbles in a tin can. Tired-looking posters proclaimed, "God is Love".

Despite this uninspiring setting and our amateurish operations – there was no fancy equipment, not even a telephone, and our records were kept in shoeboxes – the advice office fulfilled an indispensable function in the coloured and black communities. It was known as a place where assistance could be found, not in the form of handouts but in more empowering ways. We engaged with people on a personal level, heard their stories and took practical or paralegal steps to give them even the smallest measure of control over their situations. Sometimes the helpful action was as small as a phone call to an employer or a creditor made from a callbox or our own homes, or a letter written to a state department on a client's behalf. Few of our clients had access to telephones and many were illiterate.

Most white South Africans, if they knew about the Black Sash at all, would have associated it with anti-apartheid demonstrations and viewed it with suspicion. Very few would have been aware of this other branch of Black Sash activity, carried out behind the scenes through its network of advice offices. Established first in Cape Town in 1958 and later in major centres all over the country, the advice bureaux were the agencies through which the Sash engaged with the poor, helping them steer their way through the debilitating circumstances of poverty and proscriptive legislation. Through this work we gathered an enormous wealth of information and insight regarding the life of the oppressed and the apparatus of the oppressor. The advice offices really were the engine room of the Black Sash and it was a matter of pride to the organisation that its political demonstrations and social justice campaigns arose not out of sentiment or idealism but out of solid information and analysis, gleaned from its own hard work.

While I was by nature drawn to the principled actions and expressive dynamism of the Sash's public activities, my training in welfare drew me equally strongly to the advice office. Apart from paid interpreters, advice office staffers were all volunteers. Most of us had other jobs during the week, so we worked on Saturday mornings on a roster system.

One cold morning in August 1976 I was on duty interviewing clients at a rickety school desk in the crowded St Clements hall, when I became aware of a keening sound at the table next to mine. The woman being interviewed was rocking to and fro in her chair and was clearly distressed. There was no privacy in the hall and the sad sound was beginning to make all other conversation impossible. So we took her into the church where we shut the door, and in between sobs she told us her story. Her daughter, a deaf teenager with speaking difficulties, had disappeared. She travelled regularly by rail to a special school in Umtata (now Mthatha) in the Transkei, a long and convoluted journey that involved changing trains. Her mother always asked the train guard to look after her, but this time her daughter had not arrived. She had reported the disappearance and was now frantic with worry. We decided to accompany her to the railway station to see if we could expedite her search.

The station had Victorian gables and lofty waiting rooms with benches marked "Whites only". Steam engines were still pulling trains on this line and the metallic smell of railway smoke hung in the air. The booking clerk directed us to the railway policeman whose dingy office adjoined the shunting yard. The official knew of the case. Smug with his Brylcreemed hair and his comb in his sock, he proceeded to assure us that the bureaucratic process had been followed to the letter. Dockets had been made out in triplicate and sent up and down the line. I couldn't help picturing these useless notes being dropped from engine cab windows as trains flew through remote rural stations, perhaps to be picked up by a porter or more likely, the wind. We pressed him for further information. No, no attempt had been made to speak to anyone on the telephone, the civil police had not been summoned, and the railway guard who had undertaken the custody of the child had not been interviewed. Instead we were treated to a tirade on the inefficiency of railway officials in the Transkei and the unreliability of blacks in general. Then his hectoring took on a salacious tone as he lent over the desk towards my colleague and me. "I needn't tell you what I think has happened," he said with a wink. "She is probably ... you know..." and he resorted to hand gestures to imply a buxom lass, nodding in the mother's direction. I was appalled by his insensitivity and resented his conspiratorial tone. The mother gave no indication that she understood his innuendo but we all rose and left his office.

Outside, trains shunted back and forth, belching clouds of grey smoke. We were getting nowhere, so we shepherded the mother back to the advice office, where we decided that the best route was to alert the press. We assured her that the story of her daughter's disappearance would be made a top priority and immediately got in touch with the local newspaper correspondent, who was a member of the Black Sash, and she distributed the story as widely as she could.

Returning home to my own children that afternoon, I knew just how frantic I would have felt if one of them had disappeared. I also knew that the disappearance of a white child would not have been treated with the same callous lethargy as we had witnessed that day. The case had a deep effect on me. I could not imagine what it must be like to have so little control over one's own life.

The following Monday morning we heard that the girl had been found in safe care in a small town between Grahamstown and Umtata. Someone had read the story and alerted her rescuer. She was unharmed and able to proceed to school. Five years after this encounter, the girl and her mother visited us at the advice office again. She had finished school and trained as a dressmaker and we were able to put her in touch with a potential employer.

The Sunday morning following the incident, Malvern and I went to lunch on a farm in the district. The girl and her mother were in the forefront of my mind as we drove out of town under a vast winter sky. In the distance the blue humps of the Amatola Mountains loomed, and flame-coloured aloes, like candelabra, illuminated the rocky landscape. As we turned off the tarred road onto a bumpy track, a leguan slithered across our path. It was the first one I'd ever seen and with its scales and mighty tail I thought we were meeting a crocodile! We passed a cluster of small labourers' houses and a trading store before reaching the farmhouse.

The large homestead smelt of polish and wood smoke from a roaring fire in the grate. Ornate dark sideboards and comfortable old sofas furnished the rooms while bearded ancestors and women in poke bonnets looked down from oil portraits on the walls. Our hosts were charming and lunch of guinea fowl and venison was splendid. The talk was of crops and the weather, children and schools. Plates and glasses were whisked away by a silent army of maids summoned by a bell that dangled from the ceiling above the dining table. Looking out from the farmhouse windows towards the distant mountains, I was struck by how dislocated we were from the shack dwellers and their problems. We toured the lands, saw exotic birds imported from faraway places and buck leaping in the veld. This farmer, like others in the neighbourhood, was beginning to turn his attention to the American tourist trade. We talked about "the staff" and, while feudal, it all seemed humane. I participated with enjoyment and ease in the pleasures of the day, and though anxiety about the lost girl nagged at my mind I behaved myself well, knowing it would be inappropriate to introduce "politics" on such a day.

So often, even in so-called liberal circles, the mere mention of words like "township" or "blacks" was considered political and therefore off limits. Many English immigrants, enjoying a lifestyle more affluent than they could have dreamt of in Britain, preferred to keep their heads in the sand, and sometimes even those who professed themselves supporters of the Progressive Party or the Black Sash made remarks that showed their liberalism to be merely skin deep. Someone would avoid a certain supermarket, for instance, because it was "too full of blacks". Once at a very convivial dinner party, at which the wine had been freely flowing, a fellow guest greeted my "political" comments with the advice, "Go back to England where you belong!"

After our day on the farm we hurried back to town to attend a service in the coloured recreation hall to pray for the Reverend Allan Hendrickse, who had been detained. In the 1980s Hendrickse would become an MP in the tricameral parliament and be seen by many as a sell-out, but in the mid-1970s he was a symbol of the struggle. The hall was packed with people of all ages, from grandmothers to infants, and there was a feeling of anger and tension in the air. A mere scattering of whites was present, mainly nuns. We felt honoured to have been invited to attend by a man who sometimes served Malvern in Birch's, the local drapery store.

The recreation hall was like community halls all over the world, functional and cavernous, with that slightly stale smell of past gymnastic activity. In later years it became for me a place of quite special memories as I went there to hear stirring political speeches at the height of the detention campaign in the 1980s, and it was to this hall that Nelson Mandela would come in the 1990s after his release from prison. Malvern and I were impressed with the calm manner in which the Reverend Sonny Leon conducted the service and the message of non-violence he delivered. Nevertheless, the Bible readings, prayers and hymns had clearly been chosen to express strong political feeling and the singing was emotional and rousing. For Malvern the atmosphere was familiar. It reminded him of powerful Dutch

Reformed services he had attended as a child. To my ear, the guttural resonance in the Afrikaans words seemed to come straight from the heart. I missed many of the innuendoes of that service, but I remember it as the first time I'd heard the phrase "white oppressor".

What a weekend of contrasts that was. Each of the events seemed so isolated from the others, the travails and concerns of the one unknown or unheeded by the other. As polarised and baffling as it seemed to me, and as distressing as much of it was, I was at last getting involved in the kind of work I felt called to, and through it, I was no longer just observing, I was becoming a part of it all.

At the end of 1981 Gill and I closed our nursery school. The Grahamstown schools were beginning to introduce their own pre-primary classes and in time our little school would be obsolete. It was a good time to shut our doors. But I was not long without a job. I was approached to become a social worker at GADRA, the Grahamstown Area Distress Relief Association, a non-governmental welfare organisation, and since it was a mornings-only position it suited my family commitments. Our children were all well into their school careers by now but still needed a great deal of fetching and carrying in the afternoons.

I was employed in the advice section, where I stayed for 12 years until 1994. In winter I shivered in my prefab office next to the beer hall in Fingo Village and in summer it was an oven. What a far cry from my neat little centrally heated office in an Oxford hospital! Working mornings only was a mercy, as I sometimes felt overwhelmed by the demands. Our clients were almost exclusively black and engaged in endless struggles with hunger, homelessness, overcrowding, unemployment, alcoholism, drug abuse, rape and domestic violence. We did not at that stage see Aids sufferers, nor children who had been raped – though perhaps in those days we were simply not recognising the symptoms of either. It was a kind of war we were waging, not just against callous government policy but most often also against an obstructive and vindictive bureaucracy. South

African welfare services and benefits were heavily biased in favour of whites, leaving us with little professional backup.

GADRA received no state subsidy, depending entirely on donations. Over the years we tried to change and modernise the old-fashioned name but to no avail. The community we served, not to mention the donors, had always used the acronym GADRA and wanted it to stay. Two other agencies to which we were linked bore the old-fashioned names of the Cripple Care Society and the Civilian Blind. These and other aid societies were run by stalwarts in the white community. One of my young colleagues once remarked, "Everyone in welfare is so old!" They were indeed a dying breed.

GADRA was founded in 1959 in response to a mayoral appeal. It could have been a flood, the ongoing drought, or perhaps simply the overwhelming miasma of poverty. Prior to this there had been ad hoc charitable activity in Grahamstown, carried out by the churches and the Good Samaritan Society. Early in the century there had been an Englishwoman who, according to legend, rode a large white horse through the townships dispensing medical advice and assistance. Later the wife of a law professor started soup kitchens and a school-feeding scheme when she learnt that children were fainting at school because they were inadequately fed. In the 1970s a bursary scheme was launched, modelled on the African Scholars' Fund in Cape Town. An ageing Jesuit priest administered the bursary fund from boxes stored under his bed. Humble beginnings, but in time GADRA became a very efficiently run outfit with a welfare number, a constitution, and a strong team effort uniting the three sections: Advice, School Feeding and Education.

Fresh to South African welfare work, I was at a distinct disadvantage when practising what is known in the jargon as cross-cultural social work. For one, I could not speak isiXhosa. Apart from the fiendishly difficult grammar, my limp English tongue could not master the clicks and glottal stops. I had to depend on interpreters who, I discovered, tended to supplement my advice to a client with sixpence worth of their own for good measure, which could muddy the waters somewhat. Fortunately my closest colleague, an experienced social worker, was fluent in isiXhosa. Adrienne Whisson also lectured at the university, was a member of the Black Sash and had a feisty, clear-sighted approach that was a great asset in our line of work.

I was also unfamiliar with many cultural nuances and had much to learn. Fortunately I was encouraged and aided by an ex-school principal who worked in the office. She was especially supportive when I found myself having to let go two of our colleagues, one after the other, the one for drunkenness and the other for theft. Mrs M, as we fondly called her, had many money-saving tips which she dished out to the clients, one of which was to use bicarbonate of soda instead of expensive deodorants. I wondered whether on a hot day one mightn't start to fizz!

My colleagues were all helpful in interpreting the township world to me. The first time I was told that a client would not be appearing for his interview because he was "late", my irritation proved quite inappropriate as it transpired that he was in fact deceased. I was baffled and amused by expressions like "sit-in lover" for a live-in lover and "chasing the century" for someone who was growing old. One passionate letter we received waxed biblical in its exhortations: "Yes, let us go on, my faithful learnards. Rome was not built in a day. For this God is our God forever and ever. He will be our guide even unto death. Diamonds can be picked up," it concluded, "but faithful people are rare." Another letter concluded with the Quaker phrase, "Let us hold this problem up to the light."

One young graduate social worker was a South African Barbara Cartland in the making. Her flamboyant write-ups on her clients sometimes made me blush to remember my own purple prose, of which my supervisor at the Radcliffe had so disapproved. "From the client's history it would seem," went one report, "that she is married to a quarrelsome, impoverished man and has been shut up in this small gloomy heap. Her nights pinned down by fear of what might happen and having to be indebted to her husband's changing moods she is now only imprisoned by the need to escape this brutal life." Another report, describing a visit to a paraplegic, read, "A bright exotic home with the bulge of the client's body entrapped on the couch. Fragile face and jaw line is raised in a gallant obstinate determination. His fathomless eyes seem to mourn all the inexplicable cruelties and sorrows of time and the world." This same girl once complained about our rather meagre salaries, telling me, "It is alright for you, you have a fat cushion to lie back on."

I never ceased to be amazed by the variety and inventiveness of the strategies people devised to survive. They collected and sold old bottles, newspapers, coal, manure, pine cones, wood. Snacks and sweets were sold at school gates, catching children on their way in and out. Knitting, sewing, leatherwork, doing someone else's housework, looking after babies, "mudding" wattle-frame houses – the list was endless. Sadly of course it also included petty burglary and prostitution.

Many households were headed by women, who were generally acknowledged as the backbone of the township community. Lack of employment in Grahamstown, together with the migrant labour system, meant that men left home to seek opportunities in the mines and elsewhere. Some women's organisations taught simple skills to improve the standard of living and humanize the environment. During home visits I was struck by the cleanliness of so many houses. They were often cramped and inadequate, with leaking roofs or badly fitted doors, yet people scrubbed and cleaned even though water had to be fetched from a tap down the street. One of our clients had received financial compensation for the loss of a leg in an accident, enabling the family to put a new roof on their house. "When I look at the roof," his mother said, "I see my son's leg."

It was a revelation for me to learn about the broad-based system of African kinship and the density of social networks. Extended webs of interdependence meant that sometimes relatives of three generations lived in the same household, helping out with food and money and providing support in emergencies. Voluntary groups such as churches, mutual aid associations, women's groups and rotating credit clubs formed part of the supportive networks that helped relieve people's financial and emotional burdens. When the state casually disrupted or intervened in the lives of black people it was usually with no regard for the crucial role played by supportive social networks such as these.

A pressing concern in the Eastern Cape was the resettlement of people. The nationalists had a grandiose plan, not unlike that of King Canute, the Viking King of England, who infamously attempted to stop the tide from coming in. "Go back, you black flood!" the ruling party seemed to cry as they set about removing black people from South Africa and relocating them to a series of ostensibly independent states. Here they would enjoy so-called autonomy, while in fact real power would remain entrenched in white South Africa. As early as 1917, even the great internationalist Jan Smuts had said in a speech delivered in London, "In South Africa you will have in the long run large areas cultivated by blacks and governed by blacks … while in suitable parts you will have your white communities, which will govern themselves separately." This meant, of course, resettling people from where they had migrated to the cities and towns and dumping them far from any sources of livelihood and support. It was a cruel and deluded project that caused untold misery, witnessed, among many other things, in the appalling malnutrition figures of the next few decades.

Two of the new homelands were located on our doorstep. When the Ciskei became "independent", a new capital was built at Bisho (now Bhisho). A series of heavy buildings, a cross between Star Wars and the Weimar Republic, rose like bunkers in the veld. Among the finishing touches were parking spaces marked for VIPs, and others for VVIPs. But like the fictional Toy Town of my childhood, with its cardboard houses and strutting, opinionated characters, this façade had no substance. For many of us it was a symbolic moment when, in the midst of the so-called Independence Day parade, the towering flagpole with the new Ciskei flag fell down like a toy.

One of my first visits to a resettlement area was in the early 1980s when I went with two other Black Sash members to Kammaskraal, beyond Peddie to the east of Grahamstown. People had been moved there from the coastal areas of Kenton and Alexandria. A general invitation had been issued to the white churches of Grahamstown to participate in a communion service with the people of the area. We travelled in a small cavalcade of cars, up and down rutted dirt roads on a beautiful spring day. The countryside was greening and the hills rolled towards the distant coast. It seemed a lovely pastoral scene, but of course it was completely undeveloped – except for the rash of government-issue lavatories that greeted us like upended tin coffins as we neared the settlement. Clearly, a further influx of people was anticipated. Such houses as had been erected were made out of packing cases and tomato boxes. Astonishingly, some had flourishing gardens helped by water from a nearby dam.

The multilingual ecumenical service took place beside the road on a hilltop. There was a preponderance of women and children. Some wore their special church uniforms of starched white hats, scarlet jackets and black skirts, some were in frilly dresses and smart hats, some in tattered clothing. When the peace was given, the entire gathering leapt up and danced. Then the communion wine came, in chalices and broken cups, and we all lined up at the side of the dusty road. As we left there were knots of people wandering off over the hills, shouting, singing, dancing, in an air of medieval festivity. It reminded me of a day early in our marriage when Malvern and I participated in a Ban the Bomb march to the nuclear power station at Aldermarston in Berkshire, England. A huge cross section of people, from Christians to anarchists, hippies to housewives, sang and danced their way down country lanes, banners held aloft. Among the high hedges it was impossible to see where the crowd began and ended. Such expressions of the human spirit, with their combination of grit and joy, have always had the power to stir me and on that day at Kammaskraal I was again amazed by the resilience the people displayed. Transplanted far from the lives they had known, in makeshift dwellings exposed to the extremes of Eastern Cape weather, yet they participated joyously in a church service with visiting strangers.

Resettled, repatriated, removed; dumped, displaced, forgotten – these words were all used to describe the many millions of South Africans who were forcibly removed in pursuit of the policy of separate development. In the Eastern Cape their need added significantly to the strain on the already heavily burdened and under-resourced region, and our advice offices and welfare organisations felt the impact too.

One of our long-term goals at GADRA was to change the mindset of those receiving aid, from passive dependency to a more proactive engagement. My predecessor had started asking recipients of food parcels, euphemistically called "rations", to offer some small token in return. They could work in the allotment behind the offices where spinach was grown for distribution with the food parcels, or cut up stockings to fill cushions for energy-saving wonder boxes – a home-made device used to keep saucepans warm.

In a further effort to impart self-help skills we introduced a development component to our work and gave it the isiXhosa name Masakhane – let us support each other. A volunteer introduced us to the deep-trench method of gardening and encouraged people to make water tanks and erect wire netting. This style of gardening suited the Grahamstown area, where water was a scarce resource. With plenty of mulch and compost, the method required less land, labour and water, and had the further advantage of recycling biodegradable rubbish. From small beginnings our gardens expanded and in time people started seeking help with their own gardens. When Betty Davenport, another staunch Black Sash member and a very able craftswoman, joined our staff we diversified our development work to include sewing groups and other practical activities.

Our school-feeding scheme was managed by an indefatigable and courageous stalwart. Margaret Barker was the wife of the Anglican Dean and also a Sash member. She delivered food to a number of township schools daily in her kombi, continuing even through the late-1980s, when school buildings were being burnt down in protest against the education system. Most of the time she had to contend with heavy army and police presences in the townships.

The feeding scheme was often given donations of food, an excess from a student function perhaps or a surplus of carrots from the market. Once Margaret and I drove out to a nearby farm to collect a donation of pineapples. We took baskets and boxes and a pair of old gloves for the prickly work of loading the fruit, but when we arrived we discovered that we were also expected to pick the pines ourselves. Margaret didn't falter, and armed with one glove each we set to. Fortunately a group of farm workers arrived in time to lend their skilful hands and soon our kombi was loaded with a bountiful harvest.

Reconciling the public's idea of gifts with our policy of becoming less of a hand-out agency was quite a balancing act, but over the years we managed to get our message across. Nothing, thankfully, ever rivalled an event I took part in shortly after arriving at GADRA. A service organisation wishing to donate food parcels asked us to identify our "most needy" cases, who would personally receive the gifts at a handing-over ceremony. It was difficult enough just deciding who the most needy were, but then we discovered that the venue for this proposed display of charity was to be an industrial site, which entailed a considerable walk. Some of our clients were frail and elderly and a few were disabled. The reason for selecting this out-of-the-way venue, it transpired, was that GADRA had a reputation for being political and the donors did not want to attract too much attention. That word again – I could hardly contain my frustration. "Political!" I spluttered. "What does that mean?" My more seasoned colleagues remained poker-faced and we proceeded with the bizarre scene. Names were called and people received their parcels with humble bob curtsies, after which they sang a hymn of thanks and had their photograph taken with the donors. That event bothered me for a long time – it seemed to be part of the very paternalism we were trying to eradicate.

A lot of GADRA's work involved pensioners and one of our campaigns targeted the poorly organised pay-out system in which people waited in long queues for up to 10 hours at a time to receive their grants. Waiting in bad weather or in the fetid atmosphere of a community hall was an exhausting ordeal for the elderly and disabled, and in some instances people fell ill or even died in the queue. It was not uncommon for those in need to start standing before sunrise, not only to be certain of an early place but also to ensure being served before the money ran out. The latter happened from time to time and then pensioners had no choice but to queue again the next day. It seemed to us a simple matter to streamline the method by staggering the pay-out days: old age on one day, disability on another, and so on. We also proposed better systems of queuing. A tiresome bureaucratic tussle ensued. GADRA and the Black Sash collaborated on this campaign, attending endless meetings with officials. The changes came slowly, but at last our ideas were adopted.

Pension fraud was commonplace, often perpetrated by unscrupulous family members or neighbours posing as procurators, with the result that many who were incapable of walking insisted on collecting their money in person. On one occasion I saw a young disabled man crawling to collect his grant. Once a year all pension holders had to present themselves to verify that they were still alive. On such days we witnessed Hogarthian scenes of the halt, maimed, aged and blind shuffling along, supported by sons or daughters, transported in wheelbarrows or carried on someone's back.

I was once asked to help the Family and Marriage Association of South Africa (FAMSA) with the case of an old man from Malawi who had spent the better part of his life as a waiter in a Grahamstown hotel. He had fallen ill and was unable to continue his duties. It was difficult to establish exactly how old he was but his face was lined, his hair grizzled and he walked with a shuffle. The hotel gave him no pension, feeling that they had fulfilled their obligation by caring for him while he was sick. With no chance of a state pension, he wanted to return to Malawi. I was reminded of the words of a Mozambican migrant worker to an advice office volunteer in the Transvaal: "You pick us like grapes, suck us dry and then throw us down."

We were able to contact the old man's family and arrange a passport, then sent him on his way with an air ticket provided by the Black Sash. In Port Elizabeth and Johannesburg he was met by Sash volunteers who provided overnight accommodation then steered him towards his connecting flights to Malawi.

While all these arrangements were being made there was the matter of the old man's luggage. He carried all his worldly belongings in two beaten up hospital sterilising boxes that we knew would never survive a trip to Malawi. But he was adamant that they must go with him and even when FAMSA produced a suitcase, he would not reconsider. So off he set from Grahamstown with the boxes held together by string, but in Port Elizabeth they were prised off him with promises that they would be sent on. In due course there was a letter of gratitude from his daughter. "My father was lost and destroyed," she wrote, "but now because you forewarned he is safe and sound. When he left Nyasaland it was a dense forest with a village here and there, now it's a new city." We could just imagine the old man's bewilderment. The letter ended with a request for the boxes. "I would like to make my Dad happy in his old age if it is the last thing I do before he moves to the next world." Alas the boxes never reached Malawi, but at least his worldly goods in sturdier packages, did.

Once a man who had spent a lifetime in a psychiatric hospital appeared on the GADRA doorstep. He had no family or friends and we had to organise a life for him, which involved getting an identity book, clothes and somewhere to live. When his story appeared in the newspaper we received offers of clothing and food from white Grahamstonians, but some were not prepared to bring these donations to our office. The township was an unknown world to them, an alien place where conditions were too frightening to contemplate. For many white South Africans the real fright they were avoiding was the unspeakable poverty that would meet their eyes. Local poet Lungile Lose, standing among the densely packed shacks of the township and looking over towards the whitewashed town, captures the chasm between the two worlds in his poem *Tantyi and Town (distant view)*.

> A racked house
> Faces me boldly,
> Ponds of water here and there
> Make one screw one's nose.
>
> Brown, rusty – most houses,
> Paint here and there.
> White smoke tries unsuccessfully
> To conceal the houses from heaven.
> Dark heavy clouds hover above Tantyi;
>
> Foamy white clouds dance above town.
> All the houses are white.
> Did it snow over there?
> I wish it would snow here too.

At GADRA and in the Black Sash advice office we sometimes despaired that the weight of poverty would ever be lifted from people's backs. This was especially so when our work tended to be merely palliative. In the Black Sash, at least, our activities were always aimed at bringing about social change and our efforts were buoyed by positive activism. At the end of a day's work at GADRA, if there were no meetings to attend, I would sometimes take Garp, our black Labrador, into the hills behind our house. There amongst the Australian gum trees and the white arum lilies beside the dam I would take deep breaths and clear my mind, burdened by the hardships I was witnessing at work but at least feeling less paralysed by confusion and guilt.

At home I had the help and support of Hilda Faltein, who started work with us as a young woman in the late 1960s. She worked full time for many years and then continued to come in as a part-time char. Our children loved her and related to her as a second mother, especially when their own was rushing off to endless meetings. I always tried to keep mindful of Hilda's circumstances and conditions of employment, especially as the plight of domestic workers was a recurring theme in the advice office.

With no legislation to regulate the employer/employee relationship in this sector at that time, workers were universally – and sometimes grossly – exploited. Long hours, poor wages and unreasonable expectations were commonplace. I dealt with a case where a worker was left in charge of a small child who caught the flu. She was dismissed on the grounds of neglect, and the employer was intent on deducting from her final wages the price of the cough medicine and the cost of the visit to the doctor. I managed to persuade her not to take such gratuitous action, but this small victory made little difference to the dismissed worker's plight. One employer, giving me a catalogue of her worker's misdemeanours, grumbled, "She's becoming too white!" A similar attitude was revealed in an advertisement in the Situations Vacant column of the *Grocott's Mail*, placed by a well-meaning employer: "Domestic worker looking for full-time employment. Owner leaving town."

One worker complained that she had too little time off to go to church on Sundays. "They won't bury you if you don't attend church!" she worried. She told of how the maids (there were three of them in the house) were kept waiting for what seemed like hours while dinners were in progress. Her employers were well-known members of the Grahamstown community with a high profile in the Progressive Party, so it was a tricky interview the advice office worker had with them, but more free Sundays were negotiated. Years later, when this employer was old, widowed and quite disabled, he told me during a bedside visit of his gratitude to this same domestic worker, not only for her years of service but also for the many intimate things he now needed her to do for him.

The house I'd grown up in had a small maid's room upstairs and electric bells, even by the bath, wired to numbered hammers in a glass-fronted box in the kitchen, but these belonged to a bygone age. There was no maid and no ringing of bells when we lived there. My mother employed a series of chars with whom she often sat down and had a cup of tea. There was Mrs Shaw, whose husband was a lorry driver and whose passion was ballroom dancing. And Agnes who had spent her early life "in service" in a large country house. I think I grew up respecting them as I would anyone else who came to tea. And yet – I have an embarrassing memory. When Agnes was new in our employ I once unpacked our silver and glassware from the dining room cupboard and proudly displayed it for her benefit. It seems a strange thing to have done.

Still, when I arrived in South Africa I had very idealistic intentions as an employer of domestic help. I vowed never to use the word "servant" or to demean older women and men by calling them "girl" or "boy". I was determined that my employees would be treated as equals and regarded with dignity. I fear that my practice did not always match my principles.

Once when English friends came to visit, they confided in us about a conversation they'd had with Hilda. When they had remarked to her that she must be very glad to have such good employers, her response had been rather lukewarm. I was taken aback. Was it just a bad day, or did I have cause to be ashamed? I reflected on how hard it must be to care full time for someone else's home and children. On top of these demanding duties, domestic workers still had their own homes and families to care for and their own worries to contend with. Considering the indispensable contribution they made to the middle-class lives of others, one had to concede that the wages they earned and acknowledgement they received were nowhere near an adequate recompense. Small wonder that Hilda sometimes arrived at work in a dark mood, which our children called a "munch" and I confess I found irritating. Other friends from England once pointed out that I often had conversations in front of Hilda without including her. No doubt Hilda's dignity sometimes hindered her from speaking up, but at other times she was not, as my mother would have said, "backward at coming forward," and she told me in no uncertain terms when she felt something was not right. This could lead to a robust debate, or it could make me feel annoyed and guilty.

In 1980, Black Sash member Jacklyn Cock produced a book about domestic workers called *Maids and Madams*. Her research was done mostly in the Eastern Cape, which she called "the Deep South". The book contained some revealing interviews. "They call me one of the family," said one worker. "How can they say that?" "Holidays?" said another worker sardonically; "I go with the family to the seaside and work harder there than I do when they're at home!" "I live on the smell of their meat," said yet another. Discussion of Jackie's book at a Grahamstown Black Sash meeting caused quite a furore, as some members became defensive about their own treatment of the women who worked for them. A slide and tape show of the book was aired around the country, and abroad by organisations such as Christian Aid. My voice, with its English accent, was used to represent the madam!

The subject of domestic work was very controversial and legal measures to regulate the practice were long overdue. It was no surprise in the early 1990s, during pre-democracy discussions, to find black caucuses citing domestic work as a matter of deep grievance and hear the wish expressed that there should be no more domestic labour once liberation had come. In the meantime, however, it was the conservative camp who reacted to Jacklyn's book as though it were a threat. After its publication she began to be pestered by anonymous letters and phone calls. At times she received up to five calls a day. She'd hear an alarm bell ringing, or the ticking of a clock, or what sounded like an electronic scream. Once after a very nasty attack of encephalitis a voice said, "You have been sick; we are going to make you sicker." Then one night the lights in her house went out and there was a crash through the window. A 20cm stick of dynamite had been hurled through the window, landing on the dining room table. Police and explosives experts arrived and neighbouring houses were evacuated. Fortunately, although the dynamite smouldered for about half an hour, it failed to explode.

At GADRA and in the advice office we increasingly sensed that dynamite was smouldering all around us. The relentless poverty and deepening discontent, together with the escalating conflict between the forces of oppression and resistance, would surely soon explode. The Black Sash steadfastly stood against any form of violence but we grew fearful that the worst might be inevitable. The kind of treatment to which Jacklyn Cock was subjected became only too common in the years that followed, as the security forces tried to intimidate and clamp down on all elements of the liberation struggle.

Time out

As an only child I had vowed that one day I would have a house full of children. My mother had been an only child and my father's sister had no children, leaving me not only without siblings but without cousins too. I was determined to remedy the situation. Our four did not quite reach the vast numbers I had imagined, but they certainly filled our home. Malvern was a hands-on dad long before it was fashionable to be so, changing nappies, blowing noses and wiping away tears. Between us, he, Hilda and I fed and bathed the children, plaited the girls' hair, sewed on buttons and took up hems, fetched and carried, comforted and scolded – and attended endless swimming galas. Our children were all excellent team swimmers and Malvern was an avid supporter. I cooked meals, Hilda baked bread, Malvern helped with homework. The result was a fairly ordered and very cheerful home.

In the early days we took in lodgers to help pay for renovations to the house. One philosophy student spent most of the time in his room asleep behind closed curtains, until it became necessary for tutors and parents to intervene and psychiatric help to be sought. An American economics lecturer seemed to have difficulty communicating and related best to our cat. His silent, gangly presence in the house was depressing and fortunately he stayed only a few months. One of HW van der Merwe's researchers, a relation of the Rothschild dynasty, came for a while and she became a friend. I often wondered what she thought of her lodgings, where some of the walls were still unpainted. We also took in several English Honours students whom Malvern knew, two of whom subsequently became his colleagues.

Impecunious students often took their meals with us, which inevitably led to dinner table discussions on *Hamlet* or *Heart of Darkness*. But the point came when these debates interrupted family conversation. The children were impatient to tell their own stories and in fact we were all becoming keen to have more space. One year we holidayed in a large house in Cape Town where the children could each have their own room. A blissful silence descended, as bedroom doors were closed and each child nestled into his or her own special space. That was when we realised that they'd shared rooms for long enough.

Matthew's new room had fish in an aquarium and a shelf of books on Churchill. During his Manchester United phase it was draped in red scarves and flags. Charlotte had an old kitchen table on which she made a doll's house. She spent hours filling the rooms with furniture made out of matchboxes and tiny lampshades ingeniously fashioned from toothpaste tube tops covered in foil. Lucy would close her door and deliver lectures to the walls in a variety of voices, so that sometimes we genuinely wondered who was in there with her. Anna and her friend Fiona played at being grown-ups, mostly marching around with carrier bags full of old bills.

Over the years, troops of friends were in and out of our house. During the high school years, when boarders were given lunch on a Sunday there was never any difficulty persuading anyone to wash up. The kitchen, cosy and warm, was a great place for socialising, with apparently many an assignation made and broken there. Years later Anna complained that Matthew had seduced most of her friends within those walls. Malvern and I wondered how we could have missed this Casanova in our midst.

My real passion was Christmas. Matthew once remarked, "My mother is an activist the whole year round, but at Christmas she becomes as bourgeois as anyone." I loved baking pies and puddings, the smell of turkey basting, the twinkling of Christmas lights and decorations and the chatter of many voices around the table, where we would often be joined by friends and their families. Sometimes we chose themes. One year everyone dressed up as Victorians, another, Anna and her boyfriend organised a treasure hunt that took us around town. On Boxing Day, which was also Malvern's birthday, we usually had an open house. This meant a great flurry of cleaning after the Christmas Eve dinner, and then Malvern would make gallons of punch, which he would personally stand and ladle out the next day. Friends milled about our garden meeting each other's extended families visiting for the holidays. It was fun but exhausting. As a child Malvern had always felt somewhat cheated having to share his birthday with Christmas, so we were determined to make his day special, but sometimes I think we just wore him out.

Life in Merriman's House was varied and happy, and always very busy. If sometimes I was out of the house more than I should have been, or if schedules became hectic and nerves became frayed, we always knew that the holidays would come and we would set off into the countryside to find ourselves and each other again.

Each year in the late summer we would go up into the mountains at Hogsback and pick blackberries. These outings reminded me of my childhood when my grandmother came to stay with us in August. I would help her pick the dewberries that grew in profusion among the sand-hills of our North Country home, and we cooked jam while she told me stories of her own childhood. Years later when Malvern introduced me to the poetry of Seamus Heaney, his poem *Blackberry-Picking* brought back memories of those summers.

Now though, when I re-read that poem, it's our Hogsback holidays I conjure up. Our good friend Nova de Villiers and her four children would drive up into the mountains in her large brown station wagon, and we and our four in ours. Our destination was a stone cottage in a magnificent mountainside garden, planned, planted and tended by its owner over many years. It was a delight in spring with azalea and rhododendron, in summer with hydrangea, iris and rose and in autumn with the rusts and golds of many trees.

As soon as we arrived, the children would leap from the car to see if their favourite places and people were still there. There were the local Xhosa children, whose parents worked on the property and lived there. And there were the magical hiding places under low-branched fir trees, by the azalea-fringed duck pond, and up by the swimming pool in the orchard, nestling in natural rock. Arguments would ensue about who had to carry the luggage into the house and in which room each group of children could sleep. The younger ones always woke so early, while the older ones slept so late. There would be boxes heaped with food and Malvern would struggle to get the paraffin-burning fridge working properly. The lamps would have to be filled and the gas cooker checked. The smells from these appliances would permeate the house, mingling with the scent of wood and ash from the fireplace.

There were many feasts in that house. One particularly balmy night we dragged the dining room table and chairs outside and ate our supper in the darkness, enveloped in warmth and silence. The only sound was the distant singing of isiXhosa hymns, and apart from our lanterns, the only light came from the tiny pricks of fireflies darting amongst the trees.

Hogsback is a settlement strung along a ridge below the Amatola mountain range. Cascading waterfalls formed deep pools amongst the forest glades and the rich, fertile soil provided an oasis for many English flowers and berries. Come summertime, streams were flanked by carpets of arum lilies. In the forests there were grey parrots and the raucous cry of the loerie could be heard. If lucky, one might catch a glimpse of its scarlet wing.

Over the years we walked up most of the mountains, plodding through long grass while keeping a wary eye out for snakes. The leaves and twigs of sage bush and everlasting flowers caught on our boots and socks and their scents clung to our clothes. Matthew and his friends, like sure-footed mountain goats, would get to the top long before the rest of us. Catching our breath when we got there, we looked at fold upon fold of hill and valley stretching to the horizon, with here and there a tiny dot of a settlement. It was very peaceful and difficult to reconcile with the turmoil of the country in which we were living.

We left the doors and windows of the cottage wide open while we hiked, fearing no disturbance in the tranquil garden. But one morning when we woke and flung back the curtains, we saw that Nova's car had disappeared. Flapping around in our nightclothes we soon found it upended in a ditch. It had been stolen in the night and we had heard nothing. Without keys the thieves had connected up wires to get it started but had then misjudged their get-away route. A helpful mechanic among the forest workers got the car in working order for the journey home.

The blackberry-picking would be left until our last day so that we could take the fruit home as fresh as possible. We would set out for an area mysteriously called Siberia, where the blackberries abounded. Equipped with plastic boxes and bowls, we would pick from the berry-laden bushes, prickled by the brambles, stung by midges, burnt by the mountain sun. By the end of the expedition, hands and mouths would be dyed purple and the children's clothes would be stained. At Easter time when the blackberry pies appeared on the table, the pain and discomfort and arguments about who had not done their share of the picking would be forgotten. Instead, the juicy mouthfuls would bring back memories of idyllic Hogsback days and with them, a feeling of contentment.

Returning home was usually tinged with sadness as school, work, and the routine and stresses of reality would soon impinge. So we'd delay our arrival, stopping for a ritual picnic supper at the same spot half way down the mountain pass. Back in Grahamstown, bunches of pungent everlasting flowers on the table and bramble prickles in the laundry formed the last link with our summer idyll.

As a child in England I had always loved being out of doors and particularly enjoyed the smells and sounds of the countryside. But on holidays we had stayed in hotels and I had little experience of camping. Now in South Africa, with little money and a large family, hotels were not an option and so during many a summer holiday, we camped. Packing the car before we left was a logistical feat. We had to fit in pots and pans and tents, while leaving space for passengers too, and try to remember all the important items like toilet paper, paraffin and torches. Malvern had a checklist and was a meticulous packer, yet somehow the day before departure was always one of short tempers and flare-ups. But once we were all squashed in the car and driving towards the heat haze on the horizon, our excitement knew no bounds.

Transkei, one of South Africa's artificially created homelands, was a poor, eroded area and fraught with problems for the people who lived there in thatched rondavels hugging the rolling hills. But the coast was paradise for camping holidays. With few people around and no access to radio or newspapers, we were able to suspend the world and its anxieties. We'd drive down to the sea on dusty, rutted roads then bump over grassland to find the perfect place for setting camp. We passed homesteads with thorn hedges where pigs and chickens rootled around, noticed the odd clinic or school, and took care to note where the nearest trading store was, where our water and food could be replenished.

The smells of those stores assailed us as we stepped across the threshold: a mixture of paraffin, mealie meal, cotton, tobacco and sweat. Zinc baths, brooms and baskets hung from ceilings while racks of clothes and stacks of mattresses gathered dust behind wire netting grilles. Sugar, flour, meal and beans were all stored in large metal bins with scoops. On the shelves behind the storekeeper were condensed milk, tea and a range of patent remedies from Vicks cough syrup to Grandpa's headache pills. The children loved the bead necklaces, bangles, brightly coloured sweets, and the strange looking bits of fur, bone and other accoutrements of the local sangomas. Sometimes youths with transistor radios would sit along the road outside the shop, probably on holiday from the mines. Their city clothes were the outward sign of their migration to a new and distant life, but one could not help wondering how children of this deeply rural place were adjusting to the snares of urban life, let alone the gruelling conditions underground.

At Ndumbi we camped in the sand dunes, just a dip between us and the sea. Being great swimmers, Malvern and the children would dash into the waves and spend hours in the water. Sometimes schools of dolphins would pass by and on the far-off horizon we might see a tanker. Nothing else disturbed our view. I was a bather, preferring a gentle river or lagoon to the sea, but I loved peering into rock pools and listening to the sounds of my family in the waves. Charlotte collected small shells which she carefully preserved in cotton wool to take home and convert into dolls house furniture. I would frequently remind the family how lucky we were to be wandering on deserted beaches, when up the coast people were paying a great deal at smarter places without the benefit of this privilege. As they grew older, Matthew and Anna would groan audibly, thinking of what they were missing.

We scoured our pots and pans with sand and washed them in the sea. Sometimes it would rain and then I was always glad that everyone could read to while away the time. Malvern would peer out of the tent and talk gloomily of packing up, while I would irritate everyone with my bright forecasts of chinks in the clouds and the imminent lifting of the sky.

I especially loved the evenings, sitting around the campfire under a tapestry of stars, telling stories as we watched the embers glow. By bedtime everyone smelled of wood smoke. We slept with tent flaps open and the roar of the waves in our ears. The only footprints on the beach besides our own were those of wandering cows.

But in fact others were not far away. One night we were woken by torchlight shining on our faces and a cluster of young black heads peering into the tent. Our hearts raced as we stumbled out, only to discover that they wanted us to buy their crayfish. They had two buckets full done which they had caught at nearby pools, stunning them as they swam towards the torchlight. Of course we bought the crayfish, even though it was illegal. Then we stood for a while under the stars, watching the moon cast a path across the sea. The next evening we enjoyed our feast, which would have been exorbitantly expensive had we had it in a restaurant.

At Shixini Mouth we watched a cow with a damaged horn become so entangled in thicket that she eventually died. Then there unfolded in front of us a sequence of events as in a children's fairytale. First came the herd boy, berated by his grandmother, the owner of the cow. Then came a procession of villagers to inspect and discuss the disaster. This group was followed by people carrying knives who proceeded to skin, disembowel and chop up the cow. In the end every piece of flesh and bone was tied up and carried off in the blanket of the skin. Finally the crows and insects came and very soon there was no cow left. To us this pageant was a lesson in ecology and a parable about living without waste.

We did on occasion venture further than the Transkei for our camping expeditions, going up into the Drakensberg Mountains and Lesotho. Of course it rained more there. You can't be in the mountains in the summer without thunderstorms and rain. There were the inevitable leaks in the tent, and we would have to hold sleeping bags in front of the fire to dry them. Occasionally we got stuck in mud and had to pull up bushes and ground cover to create purchase for the car's wheels. Lucy confessed in later years that at times she was nervous of our journeying. Of course to a small girl it must have seemed as if we were heading into the wild and unchartered jungle.

One holiday in Lesotho, it rained so much that we had to seek refuge beside the Orange River in a cluster of huts behind a rough-looking inn. Basic as it was, it was a good spot from which to observe the local comings and goings. Cavalcades of donkeys loaded with panniers crossed the bridge, their drivers stopping at the inn to pleasure the girls there – or so we assumed, judging by the squeals of delight heard in the night. We watched too as the sangoma descended the mountain, ringing a bell to herald his arrival and the holding of his clinic. And thoughtfully, the local policeman arrived daily with the weather forecast, so that we'd know when it was safe to resume our journey on the muddy road. When we were eventually able to find a dry campsite we explored the area more widely, riding on ponies and discovering a cathedral-like church in a remote valley. How difficult it must have been to build it in that rough and inaccessible terrain. We stumbled too upon an isolated trading store where the South African-born manager was living in exile, having married across the colour line.

On this particular holiday, the Bells, our friends from Kansas, were with us with their four daughters. Betsy had been a girl scout and was great at making the road passable when our vehicles got stuck. Once we encountered a lorry hanging perilously over a precipice. She tried to engage the driver with talk of mountain lore such as helping strangers in a bind but all she got was a surly look. Language was probably the barrier, but it may also have been our South African registration plates. On another occasion she made us stop on the God-Help-Me pass and listen to bagpipes being played far below. Betsy was sure it was shepherds, but as the music came nearer, it turned out to be pop music blaring from the local bus.

At Cathedral Peak in the Drakensberg we camped in a lovely poplar glade with mini rapids in the nearby river. Malvern's colleague Tony Davies was with us, a trout fisherman and good companion with many a campfire story. Though the fish were elusive that year, every day had its own memorable magic. One morning Tony, Charlotte, Lucy and I set off at dawn towards Cathedral Peak, waving goodbye to Malvern and Anna who were off to hike through the Nduma Gorge. We were entirely alone except for a gang of baboons who were barking in the distance. We unpacked our breakfast picnic and cooked scrambled eggs as the sun rose over the mountain, bathing all the gulleys and jagged crevices in golden light and reaching down to the grasses below. Charlotte and Lucy, who were at the time reading their way through the Laura Ingalls Wilder *Little House* series, danced with delight. "This is a moment we shall remember until we die," they chimed. It has certainly remained in my memory as a moment when it felt as though we had the gloriously lit world entirely to ourselves.

For several summer holidays we escaped to the tiny village of Rhodes, nestled in the mountains close to the southern border of Lesotho. The place enchanted us. It has broad streets, attractive Victorian houses and best of all, lots of lovely trees. Oaks, poplars, willows and pepper trees all cast their shadows over the dry earth, shading the streets. The story of their arrival may be a myth but it is a charming one. The early burghers of Rhodes village wrote to Cecil John Rhodes telling him of their intention to name their village after him, in the expectation, perhaps, of a bucket-load of diamonds. Instead he sent a wagonload of trees. What a legacy those leafy, shady sentries have proved to be, especially in summer when the Eastern Cape sun beats down.

Here, on each visit, we'd stay in the same stone house, loving the wide verandah and cool, dark interior lit only by paraffin lamps. The children delighted in a place where they could wash their hair under waterfalls, swim in the river, play ball in the street and pick cherries in the orchard of a long-abandoned farmhouse. There were several people living in Rhodes who were seeking an alternate lifestyle, and on one trip, Betsy Bell and I baked bread to barter for fresh vegetables from some of these communes.

One New Year's Eve it began to hail, with large, icy stones hitting the roof. There was no fridge in the house and so some of these, gathered in a bucket, proved ideal for our champagne. Don, Betsy's husband, had become friendly with our neighbour, the 76-year-old Tannie van Rensburg, and returned from a visit with a chicken. The fact that it was still alive did not deter him and when he'd plucked and roasted it we all enjoyed a splendid supper. The only mistake we made that evening was not joining the people who had come from miles around to dance the night away in the village hall. The thump of *boeremusiek* kept us awake until dawn.

It was Tannie van Rensburg who told us the story of her grandfather and the mermaid. The sea, according to Tannie, washed up a mermaid as her grandfather was walking along the beach. He quickly ordered his servant to catch the creature and took her home with him. But she was sad and began to pine, so he decided to return her. When she realised she was on her way to the sea she began to sing, upon which all the other mermaids came to the edge of the water and carried her back into the waves. Tannie van Rensburg also believed that the world was flat. "If it was round," she asked, "how would we walk? We would hang down like birds, and water from the sea would wash over us."

When Charlotte and Lucy returned to Rhodes village many years later to see if it had retained its early magic, there were many more holidaymakers, all driving luxury vehicles and upgrading the houses. It was no longer possible to sit in the road as we had done, chatting to the neighbours and sipping preprandial drinks. But lines of a poem Lucy wrote showed she was still struck by the sound of "turtle and laughing dove, piet-my-vrou", and the "blanket of dark starry sky draped over hills."

For one who had arrived in South Africa longing for the tidy, cosy English countryside, these outdoor holidays in remote places helped me appreciate the very different South African landscape. I knew that we were privileged to have these opportunities, every one of which helped me identify more with my adopted land and gave all of us the chance to recharge before returning to the demands of our daily lives.

Repression hits the Eastern Cape

It was Boxing Day of 1981 and Malvern and I were visiting a friend being held in an East London prison. The visitors' room was cramped and the thick stone walls seemed to press in on us in the heat. Guy Berger was seated behind a glass panel and the closest we could get to him was to place our palms against the barrier. Conditions were not bad, he said, but all he wanted was to be outside where he could watch the progress of a day from sunrise to sunset. We were entering the time of detentions and successive states of emergency when many people, including acquaintances, colleagues and friends, would do time in service of the struggle.

Guy was serving a four-year sentence, commuted to two, for engaging in activities to further the aims of the ANC. Upon his detention he had been deprived of sleep for 48 hours, then forced to strip down to his underwear and put through an all-night interrogation session by a security policeman who stalked around him, brandishing a cane. He was subsequently held in solitary confinement for three months until his trial. He was 24 years old, a Rhodes student and volunteer in the Black Sash advice office. Later he would become the professor of journalism at Rhodes University, after which he would be appointed UNESCO Media Development director in Paris.

Following the Soweto uprising in 1976 in which black students protested against the forced use of Afrikaans in schools, the political temperature in the country rose dramatically, and the Eastern Cape was no different. The region was the home of the ANC as well as many important political leaders. Nelson Mandela, Steve Biko, Govan Mbeki and others all had

Eastern Cape roots. The Black Consciousness Movement had a strong following in the region and it was in Grahamstown that Biko, its ideological leader, was arrested in 1977. There was an outcry across the country and around the world following his subsequent death in detention, and the South African state responded by banning 18 political organisations and several newspapers. A spate of detentions followed, and for the next decade and more, they came in unpredictable waves. According to the South African Institute of Race Relations, by 1986 the Eastern Cape, which enjoyed a high level of political organisation at grassroots level, also had the largest number of detainees in the country.

The United Democratic Front (UDF) was launched in 1983 and within a year this broad-based, non-racial movement had the support of over 600 organisations – but within the same year, over half of the UDF leaders were in jail. State President PW Botha enforced a draconian "total strategy" to deal with the perceived threat from within and outside the country. This saw South Africa extensively militarised. A partial state of emergency, rationalised as a measure to "normalise" society, was declared in July 1985 and gave any member of the security forces, of any rank, the power to arrest without warrant and detain for up to 14 days without charge. This period could be extended on the authority of the Minister of Law and Order for an unlimited period. The state of emergency also sanctioned the use of military force to coerce and control the townships through curfews, surveillance and house-to-house searches. In reply, the UDF called on people to make the townships ungovernable by, among other things, barricading or trenching the streets to impede the movement of police and army vehicles.

The battle lines were drawn. Young people took to the streets, only to be met by massive police retaliation. The South African Institute of Race Relations notes that in 1985, a total of 879 people died in political violence throughout the country, with 441 of these dying at the hands of security forces. The Black Sash intensified its role of witnessing, monitoring and recording events, especially in the rural areas of the Eastern

Cape. Membership of the organisation climbed again, reaching 2 000 nationally. In Grahamstown we had a membership of 40.

Many of the affidavits we took from township residents pointed to gross police abuse and misconduct. On 21 March 1985, the 25th anniversary of the Sharpeville massacre during which anti-pass law protesters were killed, 20 people were shot dead by police in Uitenhage. The police alleged that there had been unrest at a funeral and that they had been attacked first. But an affidavit taken from a mourner tells a different story. "I saw two hippos [armoured vehicles] in front of us and another at the back near 16th Avenue," he said. "We were walking down Maduna Road. When we got close to the hippos the police started shooting. I was shot in the ankle and fell down. While I was lying on the ground the police left the hippos and came amongst us. They took our umbrellas. They collected stones and scattered them among the dead people. I did not see anyone in the crowd carrying stones, sticks or any other weapon. I was taken to hospital in an ambulance and later escaped. I was afraid that I would be put in jail."

Much of the action of the political struggle was played out on the streets of small towns far from the regular circuit of politicians, journalists and foreign observers. Isolated and poorly resourced at the best of times, these centres were rendered especially remote during the restrictive states of emergency.

Adelaide, lying at the foot of the majestic Winterberg mountains, was one such town. I liked visiting – in winter, the range was often blanketed with snow and in summer, seen from the hot dusty plain below, the mountains seemed cool and inviting. The road from Grahamstown was lined with soil the colour of rust, dark green bush and sisal trees. Now and again one would see a monkey on a telegraph pole or the flash of a meerkat crossing the road. The houses in white Adelaide had frilly fretwork balconies and large, shady gardens and the streets were lined with pepper trees and blue gums. But the town had the air of being past its prime. Across the railway line lay the township, a jumble of shacks and dusty tracks, and beyond, a swathe of modern township architecture where small square houses stood in regimented rows, presided over by high-mast electric lights.

The Grahamstown Sash visited Adelaide over the years and saw the advice office grow from a small kitchen-run operation to a properly staffed and equipped office. The delightful Sheddy Magwa worked there. His name, he told me, came from his birth in a shed during heavy rains when his family's hut had collapsed. I was tempted to make a comparison with a more famous birth in a stable – all the more so when Sheddy told me, "Somehow from an early time I knew that I must carry the burdens of my people."

Sheddy was a warm man with an infectious laugh and a face that crinkled easily into a smile. His house was made of roof irons painted bright blue. The ceiling sagged and was stained with damp. On top of a small television set were pictures of Jesus Christ and Nelson Mandela, whom he referred to as "my man". In his youth, Sheddy had gone to Cape Town, where he discovered the ANC and began proselytising for the movement in the township hostels, enduring harassment by the police and several spells in jail. By the time I met him his days of recruiting for the ANC and for Umkhonto we Sizwe (MK), its armed wing, were over and he was now involved with the advice office and the Presbyterian Church, educating rural people about their rights.

Inevitably perhaps, Sheddy's three sons left the country in 1980 and spent periods in Angola, Mozambique, Zambia and Tanzania, where one of them attended the Solomon Mahlangu Freedom College. From 1980 to 1991 the Magwas heard no news of their sons. Once when I visited in 1990, Sheddy's wife had gone to Bisho to attend a rally at which Chris Hani was to speak. She hoped that Hani might have news. Needless to say this small, frail woman got swept up in the vast crowd. She got nowhere near Hani and came home disappointed. Eventually two sons did return, with news that Zwelithemba had died in 1984, apparently during a mutiny in an ANC camp. That was a hard blow for Sheddy, who felt that he might have indoctrinated his sons. He hoped in vain until his dying day that he might hear the full story of how his son had died.

One winter Friday in 1989, Sheddy phoned the Grahamstown Sash and told us of his fears for the impending funeral of a young boy who had been shot dead by police. Conflict was feared between police and mourners and it was hoped that we could offer a restraining presence.

My friend and Sash colleague Lynette Paterson and I travelled to Adelaide the next day. A roadblock at the entrance to the town was our first sign of tension, but we were waved through. As we entered the township we passed a group of youths wearing yellow shorts and shirts. They were members of the local sports club, waiting to escort the dead boy's coffin. Funeral marshals dressed in khaki, wearing black berets and armbands lined the path to the house of the bereaved. As we approached, a lean old man stepped forward and told us that Sheddy and other funeral organisers had been detained by the police and that he, Howard Ngcetu, had been appointed to look after us for the day. Apart from a press photographer we were the only whites there and Howard stayed close beside us all day. He told us that the previous weekend in Cookhouse, police in cops-and-robbers mood had chased mourners from the graveyard and that people were nervous that the same would happen here where already a large crowd of mourners was gathering around the house.

Police often placed restrictions on funerals, which they saw as political rallying events, and with so much freedom curtailed, they often were. The restrictions on this particular funeral stated that there were to be no more than 200 mourners present and that the proceedings were to be over by 2 pm. As there was some delay in getting the undertaker to release the body, this was liable to present a problem and added to the already mounting tension. As the morning progressed, a heavy police presence encircled the house, including a *buffel*-full of policemen armed with guns and quirts – thin, rubber-handled whips. A police dog straining at the leash was paraded up and down in front of the crowd. Howard recognised some Special

Branch operatives dressed in plain clothes, one of whom had a video camera, poised to record who was present.

When the coffin finally arrived in a small truck, the family gathered for prayers in the house, after which the official procession accompanied it down the hill to the community centre. At this point the police officer in charge, Captain Gouws, unexpectedly gave instructions for the large crowd of unofficial mourners to be held back. They were not to be allowed to attend the service. The crowd surged with frustration and we wondered how the marshals would cope, but a group of clergy who had remained behind at the house stepped in and the crowd responded with amazing discipline. People accepted the restriction, fully expecting that they would be allowed to join the coffin for the committal once the service was over. For more than an hour the group did not waver from its vigil around the house. No one left; no one sat down; no incitement occurred. In the hot, dry wind blowing off the mountains the people stood their ground, face to face with the police. We were witnessing two opposing forces of the struggle in a stand-off, the threat of violence crackling like static electricity in the dusty air.

We noticed the clergy discussing contingencies among themselves and negotiating from time to time with the police. Then, as though a subliminal message had been sent out, people started visiting the tap in the yard, surprisingly not to drink but to wet parts of their clothing. Someone fetched a bucket and everyone dipped a scarf, a hat or a handkerchief in the water. Howard pointed out the tear gas canisters. With the service in the hall expected to end soon, both sides were sensing that a showdown was in the offing and the people were taking the only precaution they could. They were determined to meet the coffin at the cemetery, while the police in their turn had their orders to limit the gathering to 200. Throughout the day Lynette and I were never afraid, but at this point we felt anxious, unsure of what might happen next. A frustrated mourner might pick up a stone; a nervous policeman might use his gun. Howard's steady presence was a great reassurance.

As police vehicles began to roar off in clouds of dust towards the graveyard the crowd spontaneously began to move. Urgent words passed between the clergy and Captain Gouws, and he agreed to let them go. Some singing and toyi-toying broke out, but the young khaki-clad marshals hovered on the edges of the crowd, guiding and restraining it with surprisingly deft authority. At the graveyard entrance, the charade resumed. A line had been drawn across the dusty road and we were told that this was as far as we could go. After yet another appeal to Gouws the people were allowed in after all, but were instructed to sit against the fence 100 metres from the grave.

I had little experience of English funerals but I'd seen many a country churchyard, quiet places, neatly tended and sheltered by green trees. By contrast this open, windswept space seemed godforsaken, the ground hard and unyielding to the spade. But in the midst of the more than 500 people gathered there, who greeted the coffin with freedom songs and fists raised in the air, I experienced an intensity of feeling that I could never have known among the moss-covered stones of any English churchyard. "We are all brothers in Christ and children of Africa!" the Reverend Finca called into the fierce wind when the committal was over and he was allowed to address the crowd. In clouds of swirling dust he and Gouws thanked each other for mutual restraint throughout the day. Then, with the shadows of the surrounding hills beginning to lengthen, Gouws lined up his men at ease over to one side, from where they watched the crowd disperse. The funeral had taken the entire day. Lynette and I drove back to Grahamstown exhausted and in thoughtful mood, each glad to have had the other by her side.

Amidst this mounting tension, in 1984 Malvern and I were relieved to get away again, to spend a sabbatical leave in Cambridge. Though throughout our time there we'd constantly wonder what was happening back at home. Letters from friends kept us informed. One wrote about how the searchlights on Gunfire Hill were illuminating the townships at night, *"son et lumière* South African-style"*. When we spoke to English friends or addressed meetings in Cambridge, I felt proud to talk about the groups I was associated with and the work they were doing, and was greatly heartened by the interest and concern expressed by all whom we encountered. We were privileged to be able to escape the pressures from time to time and to tap into this vein of encouragement and support. But as citizens of the pariah nation we were often also embarrassed to be identified as South Africans. While travelling by train from London to Cambridge one day, Charlotte, Lucy and I fell into conversation with a Canadian. When he asked where we came from I said "Africa", keeping it as vague as possible. But my two young teenage daughters, born and bred in South Africa, did not share my qualms. "*South* Africa," they sang out in unison.

By the end of that sabbatical, Malvern and I both knew that we wanted to return home. In an article for the *Cape Times*, the distinguished academic Robin Hallet, who was visiting from England, wrote about South Africans visiting abroad. He observed that, "it may come as something of a relief to get back among one's compatriots, to meet people exposed to the same pressures, and above all to regain the company of good friends." He compared life in South Africa to living on the front line and concluded, "One of the great, perhaps the only, compensations of living in a pressurised society is that friendships acquire a dimension they rarely possess elsewhere, the warmth of camaraderie."

On our return, Grahamstown presented a very different scene from the one we had left a few months earlier. From our stoep we could see burnt-out school buildings where children had rampaged in protest at their poor education and being taught in the medium of Afrikaans. Security vehicles were everywhere – *buffels*, *hippos*, and the bilious, sickly coloured *mellow yellows*. The searchlights at night rekindled memories and brought back emotions of being carried as a small child to the underground shelter in our garden during the heavy blitzes in Liverpool. It was indeed a war zone to which we had returned.

The sweep of detentions extended from the regional structures of the UDF down to the smallest street committees, causing the tight organisation that had characterised the communities to crumble. Communication within and between organisations became more and more difficult and it became harder for us to know who to negotiate with on matters of communal interest. In the vacuum that resulted from the removal of genuine political leadership, the youth became increasingly radicalised and undisciplined. Often it was anarchic youngsters who became the most militant. In the Grahamstown townships they were dubbed *amabutho*, or "warriors". Some had guns and grenades and there were incidents of running battles between *amabutho* and police. One of their weapons was a *scorpion*, a backyard construction of metal pipe, bucket handles and springs, which acted like a gun and was lethal at close range.

The *amabuthos'* primary targets in the townships were state representatives such as community councillors and municipal police, and most especially their informers, the so-called *mpimpi*. Informers were often unemployed youngsters competing for tips near the supermarket. They would have been easy prey for the security police, whose offices were right next door. A nasty incident occurred when some of these suspected *mpimpi* were taken out onto a country road and brutally assaulted. One of them died as a result and the others had to be hospitalised. Later seven *amabutho* youths were arrested and four were subsequently charged with the murder. The youngest of these appeared to be no more than 10, and the oldest just 17.

The parents of both sets of children approached the Black Sash for help. The parents of the young informers were afraid to take their children back home to the township once they had been released from hospital, as nobody, not even the local social workers, who lived in the townships and were caught between warring factions, wanted anything to do with informers. The parents of the accused were adamant that their children could not have been involved, claiming that they had been sleeping at home on the night of the incident. We listened to the stories and referred people to lawyers, then tried to discuss the implications of the case with sectors of the community.

Our fieldworker, Cheryl Walker, and I set up a secret meeting with the local UDF to see if the children could be reintegrated into the community. Their days as *mpimpi* were over and they had surely been punished enough. It was a difficult meeting to arrange as the UDF leaders were in hiding. Thus we met late one night by candlelight in an empty flat, with young men we'd collaborated with in a perfectly open and straightforward manner before the state of emergency. But nothing was achieved. There was to be no pardoning of informers and no reintegration into the community. The case was a tragic example not only of what our society was doing to its children, but also of how attitudes were hardening as the struggle intensified. Cheryl and I returned home feeling defeated, realising that we had less and less influence at a time of rapidly deteriorating circumstances.

Cheryl was the first in a series of strong, intelligent and courageous fieldworkers we employed over the years, all of whom served the Black Sash with commitment beyond the call of duty. Together with some of the younger Sash members, several of whom were academics, they brought enormous analytical strength and clarity to the organisation. Most opposition groups in South Africa were being targeted at this time, leaving the Black Sash to become home to women whose radical persuasions would more naturally have placed them on the extreme left. I kept in touch with several of our fieldworkers after they'd moved on, and was especially proud when, years later, Cheryl became the professor of sociology at Stellenbosch University. By then we could laugh about some of the cloak-and-dagger situations we'd been in.

Many meetings were held under cover of darkness, always with the dread of a visit from the ubiquitous security police. A sudden knock on the door would cause everyone to freeze. I returned to the venue of a meeting once, having forgotten my car keys there just minutes before, and found myself having to whisper through the keyhole to those still meeting inside. We all got used to sheltering people who were on the run or taking people to meetings or safe houses via back roads. For a few weeks I ferried a student leader, covered in a blanket on the back seat of the car, between her safe house and her matric exams at the Nathaniel Nyaluza High School.

Inevitably the circumstances produced their quota of conmen. We were frequently visited at home by someone who at first I called Caesar, but whose name actually turned out to be Sisa. Before the struggle he had been an upholsterer in a small town near Grahamstown. He would appear when least expected, often when there was a meal ready to be placed on the table. Like a James Bond secret agent or a John le Carré spy he would always claim to have important information, none of which ever amounted to anything. A local character called Elvis once duped me into taking him to what I thought was an important meeting. Only when we were on our way and he was patting my knee and calling me "the Mother of the Nation" did I realise that he was en route to a party, for which he was already well oiled!

Detention without trial was one of the most commonly used and profoundly damaging weapons in the state's terrifying arsenal. Randomly applied, it was intimidating, cruel and disruptive to communities and individuals alike, and it did personal harm not only to the detainee but also to everyone connected with her or him. Released detainees agreed that incarceration under such circumstances was the loneliest experience imaginable and they were always very grateful for any comfort or succour received.

As early as the 1970s the Black Sash organised a support programme for political prisoners in Grahamstown's Waainek prison, providing pocket money, films, newspapers and magazines, as well as meals for the visiting families. The champion of this programme, Kathleen Satchwell, was a fearless young woman who was to become one of South Africa's Supreme Court judges after 1994. Late one Friday night when three women detainees, one with a baby, were suddenly released, Kathy drove them to King William's Town. They were awestruck to see the lights of houses and cars again and Kathy was swept up in the eruption of talk, laughter and hugging that ensued when they reached home to find that some of their comrades, who had been held in other prisons, had also been released.

On Christmas Eve one year we tried our luck by asking permission to sing carols in the prison. Not surprised to be denied access, we adjourned to a nearby hillock where we sang under the pine trees. It was a still, warm night, the sky velvety dark and covered in a patchwork of stars and the large orange orb of a recently full moon peeking over the horizon. One of the children with us shouted out, and at the prison windows we could see arms waving through the bars of the cells. Our singing had been heard.

Helping the families of prisoners of conscience – opponents of the regime rather than criminals – was the specific brief of an organisation called the Dependants' Conference (DC). A small local committee had existed in Grahamstown since 1963, but with the escalation of detentions it was becoming inundated with requests for support. Often people just needed information about their detained relatives, but increasingly their need was for assistance to cope with the effects of detention. The Reverend Bob Clarke now opened Grahamstown's first formal DC office and in collaboration with them we established a process for the debriefing of ex-detainees. This project, masterminded by two remarkable Sash members, Priscilla Hall and Marianne Roux, made it possible for detention data to be systematised, trends to be identified and, as always, our campaigns to be informed by hard fact.

Over a ten-month period from 1987-88, some 200 ex-detainees were debriefed. Apart from the circumstances of their arrests and the conditions in which they were held, we also documented the physiological and psychological effects – and after-effects – of their experiences. Released detainees experienced depression, mood changes, lack of confidence and reduced trust in people, and very often backaches, chest pains, headaches and insomnia. Where possible we made referrals to the psychology clinic at Rhodes University and the outpatient unit at Fort England psychiatric hospital. If nothing else, just telling us their stories at least had therapeutic benefit.

Detention not only isolated people from their usual support groups but also deprived them of any control over their situation. Detentions often appeared to be completely random; many detainees were never questioned and very few were ever given reasons for their arrest. According to a 1987 survey conducted by the Human Rights Trust in Port Elizabeth, more than half of the people then in detention were being held for alleged membership of certain organisations, while more than a third were being held on charges that the state was unable to substantiate. One 63-year-old man from Kenton-on-Sea told me that he had been going from house to house collecting money for a lawyer to defend detainees from his community, including his own son. He collected small amounts, but then he was arrested. He was held in a small, very cold cell with some adults and eleven children who shared their blankets with him. "We asked for blankets but were not given them. The day we arrived there we got nothing to eat. The following day we got coffee and porridge three times a day. My book with the names of the people who had given money was taken from me. But we were never charged with anything and we never appeared in court."

Predictably, the conditions under which people were held were appalling: overcrowded, dank and filthy cells, inadequate sanitation, poor food. Medical attention was cursory at best. District surgeons would stand at cell doors and shout, "Is everybody all right?" or something similar and then move on before hearing the replies. Based on our findings we persuaded a judge to inspect the conditions in local prisons. It seemed to achieve little but we hoped that it would at least send the message to the prison authorities that they were under scrutiny. I never personally debriefed anyone who had been tortured, but the occasional story did emerge, and we couldn't help wondering whether some of our security personnel had perhaps learnt their trade from the infamous colonels of the Greek military Junta, notorious for their ghastly torture methods.

The Black Sash extended the debriefing project to examine in particular the impact detention had on the women who were left behind. Detention seemed to be designed to make life as difficult as possible for all concerned, and most often it was women who were left with the burden of responsibility and stress, along with the inevitable financial and emotional struggles. Frequently it was the major breadwinner who was detained, and usually his employer would stop paying his wages, leaving rents and school fees unpaid. On top of this, wives of detainees might face antagonism from unsympathetic communities. A cloud of suspicion was spread by the SABC and other media, with words like "agitators" and "enemies of the state" indiscriminately used. The old adage that there is no smoke without fire was often proffered as the only comment on detentions without trial, and where communities were already divided this could lead to vilification of those connected with detainees.

Usually they were held far from home, making it difficult for families to discover where they were being held, let alone visit them. Permits had to be obtained and transport was an added burden. Some relatives told us that they could not visit as they had nothing to give the detainee and they did not want to compound the mutual feelings of guilt and distress by arriving empty-handed. "I felt very sorry and worried that we couldn't go," one woman told us. "We tried to send money whenever my mother got her pension." Taking children to visit was particularly distressing. One mother told us, "The visit made my son cry. He couldn't understand why we left his father inside at the end. So I never took him again." Already these children may have witnessed the horror of their father's arrest, perhaps late at night and with some force.

Needing to be strong in front of their children and their curious neighbours, women developed a range of coping mechanisms. To hold back the tears, one woman scrubbed and rescrubbed her floor. Another went to the toilet outside so that her children would not see or hear her cry. Some women remarked that the experience had made them stronger.

"Sometimes I'm surprised that you can cope under so much stress," said one. "You find out how to do things, things you would never normally do. And you learn to speak up for people." On the whole the women we interviewed were not involved in political organisations themselves. If anything, the detention experience discouraged them from ever becoming involved. For such women the church was the most common source of solace and support.

In 1986 the chairperson of the Pretoria branch of the Black Sash was arrested. Annika van Gylswyk was kept in solitary confinement for several weeks and thereafter interrogated. Towards the end of her six-week detention she was given a choice: stay in detention under the new 180-day regulations and face a court case thereafter, or take a plane to Sweden. She was not told the reason for her detention nor what she would be charged with. Annika was Swedish but was married to a South African and had lived in South Africa for 30 years. She opted for release and was deported immediately.

Annika was not the first or the only white woman to be detained, but this event was particularly unsettling for me. I was a regional chairperson of the Sash by then, and of course, a foreign citizen too. As in Annika's case, my 20 years of domicile would be no defence against deportation. I became extremely nervous, turning over and over in my mind the choice she had made. What would I do?

More and more whites were being detained in the Eastern Cape and anyone involved in activities that could even vaguely be described as radical became jumpy. Documents were hidden away; small suitcases stood ready at front doors, almost as if we expected to be rushed off to the maternity ward. We became suspicious of strangers in cars outside the house and unusual clickings on the phone. One night, rushing out to a meeting, I found an empty space where my "orange bomber" should have been. My immediate thought was that the police had taken my trusty mustard-coloured Ford Escort. Activists often found their tyres deflated, and removing a car was not beyond the scope of the security police. I feared that the noose was tightening.

When I was summoned to the police station a few weeks later the news was a comic relief. The car had been found, but we would have to drive to Tsolo on the borders of the Transkei to retrieve it. There in the small police yard sat my car with blackened windows and no back seat. When we opened the doors a sweet, sickly smell assailed us: my bomber had become a dagga transporter. For weeks afterwards we found tiny seeds in the upholstery and joked about feeling slightly high from the smell.

It was a terrible time of fear and uncertainty. In June 1986 it was my 50th birthday. And while it seemed strange to plan a celebration when there was so little to rejoice about, in the end we all agreed that some fun was just what was needed. It was a Sunday – a sparkling winter's morning, with leafless branches etched against a vivid blue sky and a splash of orange from an aloe in flower. The garden was full of friends drinking, talking and sitting on the grass, and for a long time afterwards, as more and more were detained, people spoke of the party as "the last time we were all together."

More detentions

"Hullo, Rosie!" As the handsome young man sauntered past me in Grahamstown's High Street, I felt a frisson of loathing. And again, that flash of coppery yellow in the murky Kariega River returned and the cry of "Snake in the water!" rang in my ears. I maintained my composure and in my most imperious tone I retorted, "Only my best friends call me Rosie!"

Lloyd Edwards was a Special Branch operative, as friendly and fresh-faced as the boy next door, but beneath his panache lurked danger and deceit. He and his brother were an infamous pair, both undercover spies on the Rhodes campus until their cover was blown. Thereafter Lloyd continued as a ubiquitous presence in Grahamstown, propping up bars in local hotels or strolling confidently around campus. When the time came for the state to clamp down on white activists, it was Lloyd who was directly responsible for the detention of many of our friends and acquaintances.

One of these was Ann Burroughs, my co-chair in the Black Sash in the early 1980s. As most Sash members were professional women in full-time employment, we tended to elect co-leaders to spread the load. All the women with whom I shared leadership were challenging colleagues. Analytical, insightful, well informed, they gingered up my ideas, and when necessary, they were on hand to restrain the greenhorn in their midst. Like several of them, Ann was far more radical than I was and filled with passionate enthusiasm. Inevitably, people like her were regularly targeted by the security police. And she had the added distinction of having dated Lloyd Edwards as a student.

"Ex-Lover Ordered Woman's Detention," a headline in the regional newspaper proclaimed. What the report did not describe was the period of intimidation that preceded the detention. It began with a knock on the door late one night when Ann was alone in her house. She quickly switched off the lights and listened to the ensuing silence. Then she heard people quietly calling her name. "We know you are in there," they tormented her. For some time they walked around outside the house before eventually going away. This kind of intimidation was by no means unheard of. Two Sash activists returned from work one day to find a bloodied and necklaced doll pinned to their door. Marion Lacey was a radical academic who was not shy about her ANC sympathies, while Melissa de Villiers had made her name as a student activist. Marianne Roux, a specialist in labour relations and workers' rights, was awoken one night by the noise of a brick shattering her front window. Wrapped around the brick was a death threat in newspaper type saying, "Your name is to be removed from the death list soon." Her line of research had clearly earned the Special Branch's ire.

As the garden of Ann's house bordered onto ours, she started hopping over the fence to sleep in our spare room. Our nights became increasingly uneasy. We would wake every time a car stopped outside our house or voices were heard in the street, fully expecting the police to come for Ann. In the event, she was detained at her place of work at the National English Literary Museum. A phone call from a colleague informed us that a group of security policemen had arrived, produced a warrant of arrest and taken her away.

Discovering where a detainee was being held was extremely difficult but we had ways of finding out what we could. One of these was to visit the waiting room of the district surgeon, who examined prisoners and detainees. He happened to be our family GP as well, so I would go there on the pretext of needing a script for some or other mild illness, and sit paging through magazines, hoping to catch a glimpse of a detainee being brought in or out of the surgery. I would even casually ask the receptionist who had been seen that day. She gradually grew wise to my nonchalance and one day she bawled me out, accusing me of interfering in police business. Another way of tracing the whereabouts of a detainee was to haunt the police cells. Our guess following Ann's detention was that she would initially be held at the New Street police station, so we stood in the road as near to the cells as we could and repeatedly shouted her name. "Ann Burroughs!" we called. "Ann Burroughs!" Sure enough, she heard our calls and shouted back. We were soon made to move on but at least we had located her and had assured her of our support.

In due course Ann was removed to the North End prison in Port Elizabeth, where she developed a kidney infection, probably as a result of the conditions under which she was held in Grahamstown. The toilet in her cell did not work and she was provided with a bucket only after some days. Her first opportunity to wash came after three days when she was taken to the police mortuary for a shower.

Ann was one of a group of seven detainees who took the rare step of going to court to apply for their release from detention. Very few lawyers were willing to take on detainee cases but the activist community had an excellent ally in a sharp-witted and bluntly spoken lawyer with a reputation for being a tough street fighter. David de la Harpe was a hunter and falconer, and a raconteur who could stand in the pub drinking with a wide range of people, including Special Branch policemen. It was he who brought the case on behalf of Ann and her fellow detainees. As part of her application Ann used the fact that Lloyd had been instrumental in her detention. "Lieutenant Edwards and I have shared many intimacies," she said in her affidavit, "and I do not believe that he can objectively and honestly apply his mind to the question of whether or not detention in terms of the emergency regulations is justified." The case did not succeed, but a courageous stand had been taken.

We were disappointed to discover one year that Lloyd and his contingent were holidaying at the same beach resort as we were on the Eastern Cape coast. We were paddling on the river in our canoe, watching a kingfisher diving for fish and a water rat emerge from a hole in the bank, when Lloyd and his pals, beers in hand, roared past us in a boat. On another occasion while swimming in the lagoon I spotted Lloyd's partner and some other police wives lounging on the bank while a domestic worker in full maid's uniform served tea. On the tray, I was alarmed to see a gun.

There was an occasion that gave everyone in the struggle community great pleasure and inspired a resurgence of courage. Louise Vale, a Sash member who worked in informal education, had been detained. Her husband Peter tried every available avenue to get her released, from challenging the law and seeking publicity, to petitioning people in high places. All to no avail. One evening Peter went to drown his sorrows at a local hotel. After several drinks he noticed that Lloyd Edwards had appeared at the bar. Striding over to him, with a full tankard in hand, Peter struck a blow for us all by emptying his frothing beer over the surprised policeman's head. The graffiti artists wasted no time. "Down a Lloyd: Feel Satisfied!" they scrawled on the wall of a local supermarket. The parody of Lion beer's advertising slogan gave us all great satisfaction. Shortly after, while visiting Louise in Port Elizabeth's North End prison, Peter's car was stolen. We were convinced that it was not the work of an ordinary car thief.

Various other escapades gave us heart in the fight against the monolithic state. Two American friends of Peter's simply walked into North End prison one day, claiming to be Louise's lawyers. They got deep into the building before the sting was detected. In another incident the boyfriend of our detained fieldworker Janet Small dressed up as a dentist's assistant when he heard that Janet was to be brought in to the local surgery for an emergency visit. Unfortunately Mike Kenyon was himself a closely monitored activist and the Special Branch soon arrived to escort him out.

The security police were both canny and brazen in their infiltration of groups, especially on campus. Malvern and I knew several students who had been taken out for drinks and offered financial inducements to act as spies. A local pharmacist told us we would be surprised at the number of students' chemist bills that were paid for by the police. There was no doubt that a dense network of amateur spies was in operation even in this small town.

A *cause célèbre* on the Rhodes campus was the case of Olivia Forsyth. Olivia belonged to all the activist groups, where she was highly regarded for her strong leadership qualities. She had a habit of disappearing once a month to Port Elizabeth where, she told her friends, she visited an old uncle. In reality she was meeting her police handler. Olivia's regular reports must have done her so-called comrades much damage. Certainly many of them suffered harassment or detention. She was herself detained for a short period, no doubt to make her cover plausible. It was only after she had left Rhodes amid fanfares of praise that her deceit was eventually exposed.

It turned out that Olivia had been a lieutenant in the security police. Her next mission after leaving Rhodes was to infiltrate the ANC in exile. This did not go smoothly and she landed up being detained in Quatro, the ANC's prison camp in Angola. She eventually escaped to Britain, where she was reunited with her father.

Malvern concocted many a false application for masters and doctoral projects so that young detainees could have access to literature in jail. He was well respected for his political voice on campus, especially at a time when the principles of academic freedom and freedom of expression were being radically undermined. One particular protest march has left a vivid vignette in my mind. Malvern and a few colleagues were leading a student demonstration against the state's threat to university subsidies when the police, armed with batons and quirts, charged onto the university lawns. The ensuing clash resembled a football riot, but in the midst of the mayhem the phalanx of academic gowns stood firm. Malvern's thick white hair stood out like a beacon among them.

Malvern's role and image on campus made life difficult for Anna, who did her degree at Rhodes. All eyes were on her to join left-wing activities, but no 19-year old wants to be a clone of her parents and she steadfastly refused to be radical.

Meanwhile her brother was undergoing his political blooding at the University of Cape Town. As a member of the Students' Representative Council he was arrested during a mass demonstration, beaten up and jailed for the night. I was proud of him of course, but secretly relieved that arrest for political protest did not result in a criminal record. I was also grateful that he was never detained. Lucy, our youngest, confessed that she too felt pressure to be involved in anti-apartheid activities, but when she eventually went to UCT she found her niche in non-racial sport. She eschewed the inter-varsity leagues, playing tennis and hockey in township leagues instead, where poor infrastructural facilities were a small price to pay for the authentically South African experiences she was exposed to. She learnt to speak isiXhosa and made more black friends than any of us had ever had. She became active in the organisational side of sport too, and once found herself at a sports congress where she was one of only four white delegates in a gathering of 900.

I often felt guilty that my involvement took me away from the children too much and once asked Charlotte whether they had felt neglected. "Good heavens, no!" she said. "You would have been too much for us!" Our children know us too well. While Queen Mary was said to have the word "Calais" written on her heart, my children knew that they were most likely to find words like "meeting" and "agenda" engraved on mine. Often, of course, Malvern and I brought our political concerns home with us and many discussions took place around our dining room table, which sometimes bore the brunt of our impassioned conversations. There is a nasty scar where Anna once, in a furious argument about some forgotten topic, scored the tabletop with a fork. There's also a grease mark down the wall where she threw a salad bowl at her Italian boyfriend, Roberto. After she'd spent her post-matric year in Italy, Roberto came to visit. Unwisely I decided to cook my version of *osso bucco* for him. When he commented in Italian to Anna that my political activities clearly did my culinary skills no good, she threw the bowl at the startled young man.

We were proud of our four youngsters, and though we were aware that our activities put pressure on them, we felt that the diverse ways in which they were developing bore testimony to a democratic openness in our home. We dispensed many cups of tea in our sitting room to parents of young students who had been detained and were often surprised at how out of touch they were with their young. Some parents, the more politically aware, felt a mixture of pride in their offspring and outrage at the security police; but for many this was their first wake-up call to the reality of living in a police state.

At the beginning of July 1986 the security net tightened to include one of our closest friends. Malvern and I were home for lunch when a phone call came from Katherine, Priscilla Hall's elder teenage daughter. "The police are here," she said. "I think they're taking Priscilla." I went straight to the house and there in the study stood Lloyd Edwards and his henchmen, searching through her papers.

Priscilla was a formidable and highly respected activist who did especially crucial work in relation to the plight of resettled people, the needs of detainees and later, the area of informal education. We'd had little doubt that the Special Branch was watching her. She'd been subjected to a chilling campaign of anonymous phone calls and in her usual thorough way she'd kept transcripts of them all. An example recorded at 3.21am was a male voice saying, "You are going to be sorry, you bitch." Her final warning had come a few days before Lloyd's arrival at her door, when a lone security policeman had stepped into the office where she was doing some photocopying after hours. Her heart thumped as he searched her handbag and rifled through some papers. After some pointless picking up and putting down of files, he left the office with the words, "This is just a friendly warning. We don't want to detain you. You have children and your husband is in England. But these are troubled times, we are in an emergency." And then he added, "You must lie low for a bit." Priscilla felt intimidated but it was not in her nature to "lie low". In an affidavit made after the event she said, "I take my family duties very seriously, but I am also convinced of the rightness and urgency of my work, and I intend continuing with it." Her work on behalf of detainees had been invaluable; now she was to become one herself. She was told that she was being detained under the emergency regulations but was given no reason.

I felt curiously tongue-tied as we stood on the doorstep of the Halls' house and watched Priscilla being driven off in a police car. I wished so much afterwards that I had given her a hug. Katherine and Ruth, who were remarkably composed, came to stay with us, and during phone calls to Ron in Cambridge, where he was on sabbatical leave, we all dissuaded him from rushing back. For us the day was also marked by the death of our beloved dog, Sparky. Under normal circumstances we would have gone into a period of collective decline, but now we found ourselves with an extended family and little time for mourning a pet. Amongst other things, Ruth succumbed to German measles during this time and had to spend days propped up on the couch surrounded with books. Watching the royal wedding of Prince Andrew and Sarah Ferguson on a borrowed colour television set, because ours was black and white, provided some diversion. I had been a royalist as a child and still loved the pageantry. I was also glad that Ruth was being kept company while the other children were at school.

Throughout her months in detention, Priscilla was never questioned or interrogated. After three days in police cells she was transferred to Fort Glamorgan in East London, the prison where Malvern and I had visited Guy several years before. On her first night she slept in the exercise yard under the bitterly cold July stars, just a thin blanket for protection. For 34 days she was held in solitary confinement, initially with only a Bible to read. After 14 days she was told that the Minister of Justice had signed a warrant authorising her further detention. Eventually she was given privileges such as reading and study material, one letter in and one letter out per fortnight, and contact with two of the other detainees.

On his return from sabbatical Ron wrote a letter to all their friends in which he typically took the emphasis off themselves.

"Priscilla is only one of an estimated 1 400 detainees in the country (200 plus from Grahamstown alone) most of whom are black. We are comparatively well off and privileged, and have suffered no reduction of income due to the detention; the family's health, security and standard of living have not been damaged. The position of many thousands of others is far more grim, and just as arbitrary."

The National Arts Festival that year was marred by the presence of foot patrols with fixed bayonets and army vehicles cruising up and down the crowded streets, making it impossible to forget that the nation was in the grip of another state of emergency. A spate of detentions occurred in the midst of the festivities. One detainee was a student due to appear in a cabaret, while another was a daughter of the family who shared our Hogsback holidays – virtually a daughter of our own.

Melissa de Villiers was almost certainly a victim of Olivia Forsyth's devious efforts. On the night of her detention I attended the launch of a friend's book on herbs at the Observatory Museum. The museum was housed in a striking 19th century building that had once been the local clock and watchmaker's premises. It was full of fascinating old timepieces and relics of Mr Galpin's once-flourishing business. On the roof was the *camera obscura* which our children loved visiting. They would climb the narrow stairs to the tower where they would observe an image of Grahamstown in the tilting, swiveling mirror. I loved the museum too, but on this particular evening the scene struck me as grotesque. An innovative curator had arranged the Victorian furniture with flair, creating a marvellous hotchpotch of fringes and tassels, candelabra and chamber pots. The hostess was bobbing about with herbs in her hair. People were sipping wine and admiring the artist's delicate watercolours of marjoram and thyme. I admired both these women greatly, but I was on edge. I wanted to shout, "Don't you know what is going on? Melissa has been detained. We are at war!" Like the image in the mirror of the *camera obscura*, this cheerful party presented a weirdly inverted version of what I knew to be the reality of the town. I felt caught between two irreconcilable worlds.

In order to visit Melissa in the police cells of Alexandria, her mother and I had to travel to the Louis le Grange police station in Port Elizabeth to obtain a permit. An imposing tower with rows of windows, the building dominated the city that surrounded it. We entered through a turnstile to find the lobby crowded with African families also awaiting visiting permits. Surprisingly, Nova and I were left to find our own way to the top floor where the security police resided. We soared up in the lift and walked along a corridor where open doors to offices revealed banks of video equipment. There were various policemen around, stockily built, sporting moustaches and speaking in heavy Afrikaans accents – stereotypes of the South African security officer. The view from the top floor was incredible, stretching around Algoa Bay and into the far distance, where we could make out the gold of the Alexandria sand hills, which marked our destination. It was a lovely, cloudless day and we looked down on a city where life seemed to be proceeding normally, apparently untouched by political events. We waited silently, speaking in whispers, until we were finally attended to.

As we drove to Alexandria we found that we had left the lovely day behind. Dark clouds were blowing over and as we entered the small town it began to rain. Nevertheless, we had some good fortune. The young man on duty at the prison was a conscript doing his army service. Apparently sympathetic to his lone female detainee, or perhaps just not overly familiar with the rules, he allowed Nova into Melissa's cell where they sat together for half an hour – something they would not do again for the next three months. I waited outside amid the drab surroundings. The only cheerful detail was a solitary tree full of pink blossoms, anticipating an early spring. When Nova emerged I caught sight of Melissa with a policewoman at her side being taken off in a car. She was being transferred to North End prison in Port Elizabeth. Our visit had been just in time.

The only café we could find amidst Alexandria's garages and agricultural stores was inside a small general dealer. There we huddled over cups of tea at a Formica-topped table roped off from packets of cornflakes, tins of condensed milk and shiny metal buckets. There were several farmers in regulation khaki gathered at the counter. For the second time that day we felt the need to talk in whispers. Nova told me that Melissa had been treated well. The cell was small and all she had to read was the Bible. Her watch had been taken, so apart from the changing light it was difficult for her to establish the time. She had scratched a calendar on the wall to keep track of the days. She had a small exercise yard in which she could do some aerobics each day, and her food was brought from the local hotel.

Our visit to the cells in Alexandria was far better than subsequent ones to Port Elizabeth. North End prison was a bleak fortress bordering on a cemetery. Inside, footsteps echoed along stone corridors and keys clattered in steel doors. Nova met with Melissa in a small cubicle where they talked through a glass partition. I was never allowed to stay and speak to the detainee. Once, after Nova's visit, we managed to walk around the grounds whistling *Yellow Submarine* underneath what we hoped were the windows of the women's cells.

In Alexandria, Melissa told her mother that she had received a visit from Lloyd Edwards. He was not there to interrogate her but to chat in a "friendly" way – mostly about himself. He also told her who the next Grahamstown detainee would be. Nova and I felt, probably naïvely, that we must warn Tim Bouwer of his impending disaster. He was a young teacher at a school in the township, where he was active in the teachers' union. As soon as we reached town we visited his house. Tim went pale at the news but realised there was nothing he could do. He would wait. An hour later he was detained. Over the ensuing weeks his partner carefully embroidered messages on clothes, which she sent to him in prison.

Among my possessions are two scrappy notes smuggled from prison by detainees during the 1980s. One, on crumpled lavatory paper and barely legible, came from a detained

Dependants' Conference worker, Sox Leleki. "Rosemary," he writes, "I want to be visited by a legal representative as soon as possible." The disintegrating paper and the spidery writing convey something of the pathos of the detainee's lot, sitting day in and day out in prison without being charged and with no prospect of at least appearing in court. Sox's request was in vain. The Detainees' Parents Support Committee estimated that 25 000 people were detained between 12 June 1986 and 11 June 1987.

The second note is from our fieldworker, Janet Small. She was detained as late as 1988, on a winter's day when the snow on the Amatola Mountains was just visible against the skyline. It happened when we were beginning to hope that the detentions might be tailing off after a mass crackdown earlier in the year. In February 1988, 17 anti-apartheid groups had been banned in one blow. Like all the fieldworkers the Black Sash employed over the years, Janet was a model of integrity and serious-mindedness. The crumpled note, much folded and frayed by the time it reached me, read, "I feel very anxious about Sash money being spent on my salary. I deeply appreciate your support, but I think you should consider at least reducing my salary…. Looking on the bright side," she continued, "I think a restriction order [anticipated upon release from detention] may be a blessing for me. I imagine the culture shock of walking out of solitary confinement into an exuberant Sash meeting! I'm sure I'd be overcome. On a more serious note, please don't feel too anxious about me. It is very good to experience the reality after all those years of working with ex-detainees. That work had prepared me, but somehow it is different to what I expected. Not worse, different. My heart goes out to those who have been inside for years."

In Grahamstown there was no pattern to the detentions – except perhaps the signature presence of Lloyd's hand – but it often seemed that it was the vulnerable who were targeted: single women, students, people with particular family responsibilities. Very special relationships developed among those connected with the detainees, and Black Sash members were hugely supportive of each other. Judy Chalmers, Sue Power and I, Sash chairpersons in Port Elizabeth, East London and Grahamstown respectively, phoned each other almost every day. "Are you still there?" we would ask. We were part of a small but strong group bound by a common purpose and a special camaraderie. I was greatly inspired by the reserves of strength demonstrated and the resilient sense of humour that buoyed the strongest of them, come what may. When so many people around us were kow-towing to the government, this group was a lifeline.

In some circles I was viewed as radical, dangerous even. I once discovered that the mother of one of my children's friends was discouraged from friendship with me because I was regarded as a communist. I knew that this term was commonly used to tar anyone who was anti-government so I didn't much mind the label, but in truth my values were very far from the true tenets of communism. Our neighbour, an elderly man who often sat on his stoep watching the world go by, revealed just how disapproving many people were of our lifestyle when he scowled at my friends. Peter Vale once brought Nyami Goniwe, the wife of activist Matthew Goniwe, to a lunch party at our house and cheerfully called out "Good Morning, Oom" as he and Nyami stepped out of their car. The only reply he got was, "I don't greet those who walk with the black nation." A friend from university days in England visited us and was amazed to find "fun-loving Rosie turned into a wholehearted political activist". Moments like these always gave me pause. How wholeheartedly did I *really* immerse myself? In truth I knew that there was a bit of me that always held back, a part of Rosie that always hovered in the margins.

What accounted for this restraint? Was it my foreignness? Was it the spectre of deportation? Was it the fault of my gregarious nature that wished to belong to the community in which I found myself? Although as a family we all believed in the same principles and always felt generally more comfortable with others who were themselves engaged in activism, we were nevertheless also part of the white culture that surrounded us.

We maintained friendships and social relationships with many diverse people. We were "ordinary" citizens living "normal" South African lives. I could come home from work, my head full of atrocities, and step into the cool, high-ceilinged rooms of my house, full of furniture and china my grandparents had owned and the books, paintings and music Malvern and I had collected, and the disorder and chaos of the outside world would seem remote and unreal. We had friends who were apolitical. There were conversations we simply didn't have with them. We socialised with the parents of our children's boarding school friends, some of whom lived glamorous lives that were positively surreal in apartheid South Africa. There was a particular pair who would arrive exhausted from their professional lives in the city. The mother, artistic and elegant, would recline on the couch in tapered velvet pants and cloak, exotic silver bangles jangling, and talk about the buzz of city life. I loved the sophistication and flair these people brought with them and felt positively frumpish in their presence, but of my other life, the one they seemed not to know about, I could say nothing. It might as well have been another country. Did Lloyd Edwards and his ilk look at this schizophrenic muddle and decide I was not a threat? Was it my respectable bourgeois self that protected me from being detained?

Then, just as suddenly and unpredictably as the detentions of those close to us took place, so the releases occurred. Late one evening in spring, Priscilla and Ron arrived unannounced at our door. We phoned Nova and Peter and drank whisky late into the night, hoping that the release of their loved ones would follow speedily. Then one unforgettable afternoon, I heard a shrieking in the street and the doors of a kombi being pulled back. Melissa and Ann were out. The news spread and an impromptu party erupted in our house. And as always the toast was for those who weren't with us.

The restrictions imposed on released detainees were severe. Priscilla was not allowed to leave the Albany area for a year and they were all restricted from participating in Sash activities. Gradually they began to take liberties, at first secretly and then more openly, but it was a relief when all restrictions finally expired.

At the 1987 Black Sash conference in Cape Town I was unexpectedly elected one of the organisation's national vice presidents. I was not only taken completely by surprise but also concluded that I had been elected by default. The national executive was a small body that was usually made up of members who lived in the headquarters region, and I felt quite sure that far stronger women than I would have been elected, had they not been in detention or banned from holding office. Becoming part of this august body terrified me, but I decided that my appointment was important for the Eastern Cape. No one from our rather remote area had been on the national executive before, and as an area that was suffering disproportionately severe repression, it deserved to be kept on the Black Sash national agenda. In the end I loved the meetings and the journeys to Cape Town and found my fellow executive members congenial, stimulating and fun. The national leadership was always in the hands of remarkable women whom I held in awe and all of whom, I am glad to say, became good friends of mine. They were articulate, lucid and calm, and fine public speakers who were able to project both the tenacious and the balanced sides of the Black Sash's character. It was a great privilege finding myself at that level of the organisation with colleagues like Sheena Duncan, Mary Burton, Di Bishop and Jenny de Tolly. Our discussions certainly brought new perspectives to the Grahamstown experience and I think the Eastern Cape Black Sash benefited from this contact. Later, this benefit was further enhanced when our Grahamstown colleague Hilary Southall, a highly insightful and meticulous statistician and I were appointed to management roles in the Black Sash Trust.

The Sash national conference in 1988 was addressed by Frank Chikane, then General Secretary of the South African Council of Churches. In the wake of the February bannings he did not mince his words. "Those who are white still have space to cause change," he said. "If you do not use that space you are responsible for the deaths of the people." It was a direct challenge to organisations like ours to step into the breach. Chikane's challenge stirred up considerable debate, as one of our dilemmas at the time was whether the Black Sash should become affiliated to mass-based movements such as the Federation of South African Women (Fedsaw). The fact that we had remained non-aligned over three decades had probably ensured the Sash's survival thus far. Being small, we were remarkably focused and cohesive, and being white perhaps gave us a special duty-cum-licence to speak truth to white power. But given the increasingly polarised nature of our society there was pressure for the organisation to leave the ivory tower of middle-class privilege and join forces with a broad front of women. Chikane seemed to be addressing this issue directly. Emboldened by this, I and my colleague Ina Roux made an impassioned plea for affiliation with Fedsaw. In the end the conference expressed support for the federation, encouraging individual Sash members to participate in and strengthen contacts with the movement, but stopped short of affiliation. With hindsight I could see that it was the right decision. The credibility of our information and our analysis had always lain in our independence, and as the national president reminded us again, being small was our strength.

The Black Sash was anything but shy and had never shirked its duty to "use the space". The price we paid in the number of members detained and restricted bore witness to that.

Getting the message across

A distressing feature of the scourge of detentions was the number of children who were swept up in the dragnet. According to the South African Institute of Race Relations, during the eight months of the 1985-1986 emergency, 7 996 people were detained, 2 000 of whom were under the age of 16. "What kind of society needs to be protected from its own children?" the Black Sash asked.

The Sash participated in a national campaign entitled Free the Children, which eventually spread to France under the patronage of Madame Mitterand, wife of the then president, and to Sweden where it was launched by Lisbet Palme, wife of the Prime Minister, Olof Palme. In Grahamstown our contribution to the campaign was to drape a gigantic banner down the spire of the cathedral bearing the biblical words, "Suffer the children to come unto me." The banner was visible all the way up High Street and for as long as it hung there, Sash member Val Letcher and her family, all keen campanologists, tolled the cathedral bells.

One response to the banner came in the form of an anonymous letter addressed to "My fellow Anglicans," and distributed in the cathedral. "It is with deep concern," it read, "that I noticed our beautiful cathedral used by the Black Sash for a protest of a political nature. A house of God is not a place for expressing political aspirations, or its spire for political propaganda against authority. Black Sash has again shown its true colours."

The dean's response to the letter was to use the banner again, this time inside the cathedral, as part of the Mothers' Day service. Roy Barker was a man of great humility and a gifted preacher. Standing in front of this imposing backdrop with its logo of a child peering out through prison bars, he encouraged the congregation to pray for children in detention, for parents of detainees, for those who issued the decrees governing detention without trial, and for those responsible for holding the detainees. Congregants were given sprigs of rosemary for remembrance and he invited them to light candles as symbols of hope. The Black Sash distributed a Mothers' Day message in the form of a card bearing the words, "On Mothers' Day all children should be home. Did you know that in South Africa more than 1 500 children are in detention?"

The cathedral was an important home for many liberal activities and we were blessed with extremely sympathetic clergy. Almost without fail the wives of successive bishops and deans were members of the Sash and after the ordination of women had been introduced, we even had clergy as members.

In 1987 David Russell was enthroned as bishop of Grahamstown. Because of his courageous quest to draw attention to the plight of the poor, his name was often spoken of in liberal and radical circles. As a young priest he had lain down in front of bulldozers set on destroying a squatter camp at Crossroads in the Western Cape. Later he had chosen to live among the discarded people in the Dimbaza resettlement camp in the Ciskei, subsisting on the same rations doled out to them. He undertook several extended fasts to raise awareness of poverty in South Africa. Not everyone was pleased when a man of such clear commitment to the anti-apartheid struggle was elected bishop of Grahamstown, but for many it was an enormously heartening appointment. The stone cathedral was aglow with gold and purple stoles and mitres and rang with the sound of marimbas and full-throated Xhosa singing. "There will be no peace," he said in his charge, "until we share equal citizenship in this one country of our birth, no peace until there is a just sharing of the goods of the land."

People like Bishop Russell who used their voices to speak the truth were indispensable at a time of a muzzled press and a state-run broadcasting corporation. The Black Sash too had a bold and respected voice and we never lost an opportunity to speak out, whether in high-profile campaigns or in the dissemination of suppressed information. We tried the idea of a massive banner again in 1987, this time draped on the building that housed the Anglican diocesan offices halfway up High Street. We had to talk hard and fast to convince the lawyers occupying offices in the same building that the banner should be allowed to hang there. On a drizzly day we unfurled the cloth bearing the words, "Remember those in prison as if you are in prison with them," and handed out fliers bearing the same Hebrew text to passers-by. Not everyone received them willingly. I was rudely pushed aside by a high-ranking Grahamstown clergyman, not on the cathedral staff and clearly not sympathetic to their support of us. Some of our leaflets were returned to us, defaced with rude scrawls.

We once embarked on a "carcade" through the centre of town. Ten cars decorated with black ribbons and posters calling for "No More Emergencies" drove slowly down High Street at lunchtime with their headlights on. The event drew a lot of attention and it was certainly a change from our silent stands in the cathedral doorway. We spoke at schools whenever we could, but it was often difficult to get permission. The hearts and minds of the country's white children were zealously guarded, and monopolised by state propaganda. Any kind of alternative thinking was viciously demonised. Nevertheless we did find that the private schools would sometimes encourage debate and at one government school we had the occasional opportunity to speak thanks to the principal's wife, who was a firm ally.

Our younger daughters Charlotte and Lucy belonged to the Grahamstown chapter of the Pupils' Awareness Action Group (PAAG), an organisation led by young people. As their name proclaimed, they attempted to promote awareness among white scholars about the situation in the country. One evening after a meeting in the leader, Christopher Kenyon's home around the corner, the girls returned breathless and wide-eyed.

They told how special branch officers had raided the meeting, marching in and searching the house. We could picture the show of dramatic bravado, designed to intimidate the gathering of youngsters. Charlotte described how the policemen had even examined the small suitcase belonging to Christopher's pre-school brother.

We were a bit slow to realise the potential of the National Arts Festival for our awareness campaigns. I suppose we always viewed this event as a kind of holiday from the usual demands and concerns of our work, though the arts were increasingly politicized and it was never possible to escape entirely. Many artists and theatre companies were boldly using the festival to relay the anti-apartheid message, sometimes at considerable risk, so one year we decided to mount a photographic display showing scenes of repression and violence in Grahamstown. It was not very prominent but it attracted attention and we took the opportunity of selling buttons bearing human rights messages and car stickers with the words "East Cape Emergency Blues". When festival-goers were asked to complete questionnaires with comments and criticisms, someone wrote, "Since when is the Black Sash an art form?" On another occasion we organised a film festival featuring a compelling series by South African filmmaker Kevin Harris. These included a documentary on the life and work of Beyers Naude, the well-known Afrikaans theologian and rebel Dutch Reformed Church minister, and another entitled, "Witness to Apartheid", on responses to the security police during the states of emergency. The films elicited considerable interest and we counted ourselves lucky that only one show was banned.

Once, at the end of the 1980s, we held a protest during the festival. We chose to stand at night just before show time, on the steep road up to the monument theatre. As the bumper-to-bumper traffic turned into Lucas Avenue to make its way up the hill, the stream of raised headlights picked out our posters in luminous pink: "No Detention", "No House Arrest", "No Death Penalty", "No Group Areas", on and on for hundreds of yards up the hill. It was an exhilarating stand in the cold and dark, with headlights boring into our faces. The first night we stood without interference but on the second the Special Branch arrived and we were instructed to disband. We were satisfied that our bit of street theatre had made a striking visual impact on many festinos and hoped that it had given some of them pause for thought.

A popular feature during the festival were historical tours of Grahamstown. These tended to concentrate on the town as a settler city, "a little bit of England nestling in the foothills of the Eastern Cape", as the SABC described it. Visitors were shown the churches, schools and museums, the stately homes and the quaint, white-painted cottages. The Black Sash decided it was time to present the other, less romantic view, the version of Grahamstown's history as a frontier city where various cultures had settled and mingled and clashed for centuries. Thus in the early 1990s, using borrowed kombis and Sash volunteers as guides, we began to offer a social history tour which encompassed the pre-settler history of the town as well as the story of the townships.

We were surprised at how popular our tours became, especially among foreign visitors. From the top of Gunfire Hill where the Settlers' Monument stood we asked our groups to imagine the confluence of peoples in the surrounding Zuurveld, from San hunter-gatherers and Khoi pastoralists, through Xhosa stock herders to European hunters and farmers. All of them were seeking the same resources and establishing a dynamic kind of cultural and commercial frontier that might have evolved very differently had it not been for the decision by the British to demarcate and settle the Eastern Cape. The story then became a military one. From Fort Selwyn we drove our guests past the old Drostdy building and the iconic Drostdy Arch that marked the entrance to the British military barracks. From there we could look down the High Street to the Cathedral of St Michael and St George, which is built on a natural spring near which the Xhosa chieftain Ndlambe had "a great place" when Colonel Graham arrived to eject the inhabitants of the region and establish a settlement. From there we drove to Artificers'

Square, where we pointed out the neighbourhood that housed the hapless working class settlers who had been lured to the Eastern Cape to strengthen the British presence. Down the road from there, the old marketplace was a reminder that the town grew into a thriving centre of trade before the discovery of diamonds and gold in the interior sidelined it, turning it into a commercial backwater. Since then Grahamstown has been characterised by the more cerebral pursuits of education and law.

Passing through the District Six of Grahamstown, a "frozen zone" where people of various races lived in a mixed community until as late as the 1970s, we told the story of the Group Areas Act. Then we crossed the Kowie ditch into the townships. In Fingo Village, amid the dismal slums that are the result of massive population pressure and uncontrolled rack-renting, we related the events that led to the amaMfengu being granted freehold rights after the last of the frontier wars. At St Philip's church I always enjoyed pointing out the black Madonna in the stained glass baptistery window, evidence of the emergence of black consciousness in the Anglican Church as early as 1945. I also made a point of showing where the GADRA office had stood before it fell victim to the conflagration at the adjoining beer hall. Then up the hill past Makana's Kop and into Joza township, where we told the stories of the 1950s defiance campaign, the zenith of apartheid in the 1960s and 1970s, and then the 1980s revolt and the successive states of emergency. After a two-hour drive we returned to town via the Coloured and new Indian areas. It always gave me great pleasure leading one of these tours and I was fascinated each time to reconsider the history of the town and the region through a new audience's eyes.

In time, the demand for our tour grew beyond our capacity as a volunteer organisation, and we published a do-it-yourself guide, which ran to two editions and several reprints. As always, it was the hard-earned substance of our message that gave it its power. Information-gathering, monitoring and research were fundamental to everything we said or did. Our knowledge was our power and we believed that knowledge would empower others, some in their struggle for dignity, others just to throw off their blinkers.

This relentless pursuit of information was illustrated in the Sash's monitoring of all pass law cases, and until the 1990s we had volunteers who attended every political case that appeared in the magistrate's and Supreme courts, sometimes raising bail funds from friends and sympathisers. This kind of dedication, applied in a range of areas, enabled us to produce informative booklets which became widely used and respected on topics ranging from the plight of prisoners on death row to community resistance in the Eastern Cape. One, on the role of the municipal police in the Eastern Cape, was a good example of the nature of our work. In a region where fear and ignorance often prevented police abuses from coming to light, this booklet served to highlight the activities of a particular branch of the police, while also advising readers on their rights in the event of arrest.

In late 1986 we became aware of men in royal blue uniforms milling around in town. They turned out to be the new *kitskonstabels* (or instant officers), a hastily recruited municipal force attached to the South African police. Fresh from mere weeks of training, these black auxiliaries arrived in townships across the country to supplement the riot forces already deployed there, and quickly established a reputation for random and brutal operations. Their many derogatory nicknames bear witness to the disrespect with which the communities regarded them. In our area they were known as *greenflies* and *wild rats*. In fact, so unpopular were they that they often had to live in protected compounds on the edges of townships, or be deployed to areas where they were unknown. Many of those deployed in Grahamstown, for instance, were Zulus, while Xhosa men were sent to Natal. Nevertheless many volunteered for the work, lured no doubt by the combination of money and guns. Unemployment in the Eastern Cape was running at around 80% in some regions and the average wage was low.

The shifting of law-enforcement responsibility to the municipal police was part of a cynical state strategy. Under the guise of encouraging more self-determination, the state was handing over more and more unpopular functions to the black local authorities. They had previously already been given the unenviable task of rent collection. Functions such as these generated untold resentment among the people and bred internecine conflict, exacerbated by the arrival of the municipal forces. It is possible that the black-on-black and inter-tribal violence that threatened the run-up to the first democratic elections in 1994 had its roots in this situation. Our research revealed that municipal policemen sometimes interrogated suspects for up to 12 hours before handing them over to the South African Police for formal investigation. Yet they kept no crime registers, observation books or cell registers. One policeman told us frankly that when he'd heard a job advertisement on the radio for law enforcement officers, he thought he'd be settling quarrels among people, not getting involved in "robbery and assault".

Our booklet warned that entrusting lethal weapons to untrained people was a recipe for disaster. The Commissioner of Police dismissed our fears as sensationalist but there were soon several incidents to confirm our fear. One chilling event left an indelible impression on me because I personally took statements from witnesses and survivors. Four people had been killed and five wounded when three *kitskonstabels* opened fire at random on an unsuspecting household. A grandmother was listening to her favourite serial on the radio. She was sitting at the table peeling potatoes and chopping cabbage for supper, her shoes kicked off her feet. Suddenly there was a knock on the door and a cry, "Open up, open up, it is us." The door was kicked open and three drunken *greenflies* burst in. They accused someone in the house of throwing stones and began to fire wildly. Paraffin lamps were peppered with bullets, plunging the scene into darkness, and in the ensuing mayhem three families were dislocated forever. Years later when this case resurfaced during interviews for the Truth and Reconciliation Commission, it was again the poignant minutiae of the domestic scene that struck me, as well as the sudden and brutal fracturing of lives.

As the South African press became more and more muzzled, the Black Sash found itself becoming something of a conduit of information to the outside world. An unexpected interview on New Zealand radio one early morning was my first of many lessons in how to think on my feet. For calls like this we often took care to use "safe phones" that were unlikely to be tapped. We also made strong connections with embassies and foreign offices, some of these facilitated through contacts that Malvern and I made during his sabbatical leaves in England. Feeling as we did that the Eastern Cape had become a war zone, we in the Black Sash were eager for foreign eyes to witness the facts for themselves, but were frustrated when foreign officials limited their visits to Pretoria, Johannesburg and Cape Town. An exception was David White from the Foreign Office in London, who stayed with us from time to time. He was meticulous in his research and we knew we could rely on him to get the facts straight. I also grew very fond of the Amnesty International representatives who sometimes stayed with us and were always crisp of intellect and well informed.

An issue that put me in the spotlight but ended in some worthwhile international publicity was the 1986 boycott of Grahamstown businesses. The purpose was to put pressure on the Chamber of Commerce to add its voice to the demand for restrictions to be lifted and troops to be removed from the townships. The boycott was a black initiative that spread throughout South Africa and was potentially a powerful means of protest when all other avenues were being cut off. In only a few towns was the white community asked to participate. The Grahamstown Action Group coordinated the local white effort. They published a stirring pamphlet appealing to whites to "give a clear signal to township residents that we are genuinely sympathetic to their grievances and support non-violent means of addressing them." They were not inundated with support, pulling in a modest gathering of white lecturers, student leaders and some Sash members. Many liberal whites were becoming increasingly alarmed at the violence in the townships and felt that boycotts were the work of agitators. There were stories circulating of boycott defaulters being made to eat their purchases raw or having newly purchased clothes ripped to pieces. Furthermore, township shops were generally more expensive than the supermarkets in town, rendering the boycotts a cruel punishment on the poor.

In spite of these misgivings Malvern and I decided that the boycott was a worthwhile symbolic act and decided to throw our weight behind it. Fortunately it didn't last long, because shopping became a difficult undertaking. Only certain shops were exempt and they had a dearth of goods. There were attempts to form a co-operative that would buy products in bulk from outside Grahamstown, but this didn't get off the ground. Our meals became rather meagre for a while and my load of meetings only increased. Then London ITV decided to do a piece for the *Six O'clock News* on a society under siege, and they chose Grahamstown. They wished to include an item on the white boycott and asked for three people to be interviewed. The Action Group selected two articulate heavyweights who would state the political case, and then they needed someone to present the human face. That lot fell to me. The interview was to be done in our garden in front of the rockery and I carefully selected a bottle-green jersey that would look good on screen. In the event, an unseasonal berg wind blew and I ended up feeling rather hot. Trevor MacDonald, the ITV presenter was urbane and to the point but he asked none of the difficult questions we'd rehearsed. My two fellow interviewees were articulate and polished, whereas I just tried to tell it how it was. The boycott was difficult as many of the targeted businessmen were my friends, but participating was a matter of principle. The interview was shown that night in England and several of my friends and family, my aunt Miriam in particular, were startled to see me on the news. Even more startling for me was the fact that the two heavyweights had been virtually cut from the clip and all the focus was on me!

A dynamic new organisation that was also enjoying a higher public profile and helping to spread the message, was the End Conscription Campaign (ECC), which was launched in 1983 with the backing of various anti-apartheid organisations including the Black Sash. Its aim was to stop compulsory conscription into the apartheid army. Malvern and Matthew both participated, though neither became prominent in the movement. White South African males between the ages of 18 and 30 were conscripted for two years, after which they were liable for call-up as army reservists to do duties in their hometowns. By 1983 13 young men had been sentenced to prison for refusing to do military service on political and/or religious grounds. A small victory was won when the 1984 Defence Amendment Act allowed objectors with compelling religious reasons to appear before a tribunal. If non-military service was granted, they had to serve one and a half times the length of normal service.

Conscientious objection always stirs up a lot of emotion. I had read about the white feathers of cowardice that were presented to pacifists in the First World War, and I remember a distant relative being spoken of in hushed tones at family gatherings because he had appeared before a military tribunal and ended up working on the land instead of in the army. In the Zimbabwean civil war, those who left the country instead of fighting were referred to as taking the "chicken run", a term which became part of South African parlance too, as many young men left the country rather than face two years' compulsory service. After 1984 the South African Defence Force began sending troops into the townships to exert control, pitching South Africans against each other in a way that many were not willing to participate in. Registration for national service happened at school, making it very difficult for young men to escape the call-up, though somehow a few always did. In most social circles it was considered unpatriotic not to do one's national service.

Anna had a boyfriend who came from a family of Jehovah's Witnesses, and although at the time he was no longer a member of the sect, he registered for non-combatant service. This did not mean that he would never find himself in dangerous situations, however. He described an incident in which his army vehicle had been trapped in a narrow alley surrounded by chanting residents carrying home-made weapons and lethal pieces of roofing. Non-combatant or not, he was perceived as part of the occupying enemy and was in mortal danger.

President PW Botha had convinced the nation that it was facing what he termed a "total onslaught" from hostile, mostly communist forces. In this context the phrase "on the border" conjured images of boys defending the homeland against a besieging enemy. Many went to the border with this heroic scenario in mind, only to find themselves deep inside Angola or Mozambique, plundering villages and participating in operations to destabilise communities. These incursions were vehemently denied by South Africa, but their legacy was a generation of brutalised young people both in South Africa and in the neighbouring states. It was a war that had no winners. An army chaplain once told Malvern and me of his revulsion and despair when men returned to base from an expedition into Mozambique with dead bodies draped over the bonnets of their vehicles like trophies from a springbok hunt. For 20 years the South African Broadcasting Corporation ran a Forces' Favourites programme to keep up the morale of the troops on the border and their girlfriends back home. The radio presenter was awarded the Order of the Star of South Africa for exceptional service of military importance. Much more lasting than Forces' Favourites, however, is the large body of literature by young writers haunted by their experiences in the army.

The remarkable thing about the ECC was the broad spectrum of support it attracted. Many participants came from outside the usual liberal groups. Of course the campaign faced repression, its leaders were detained and meetings were banned, and yet it flourished. With its signature yellow ribbons it had a national impact and was blamed for contributing to a reported low morale in the army. Lucy had a friend who was undergoing his army training as a volunteer officer. Part of the course was entitled "Enemies of the State", which included a condemnation of the ECC. Lists of names were handed out of people to take note of in the ECC, and there was Malvern's name. Our young friend enjoyed conveying the news to Malvern that he'd made the grade. Even more amusing was the news that Malvern's photograph had been spotted in an army camp in northern Namibia. A friend of Anna's was summoned to see his colonel and while waiting in an outer office he saw the photograph on a notice board. Closer inspection revealed that it had been torn from a section in the Rhodes Rag magazine headed "Studs on Campus".

As a member of the ECC Malvern refused to participate in "dad's army", an auxiliary force of middle-aged men that went away on weekend camps to practise their shooting at imaginary enemies. He was equally unwilling to patrol schools at night with armed and trigger-happy patrols. But a civil defence option he was happy to consider was fire-fighting, so he joined the auxiliaries. He was issued with an overall, which looked as though it was meant for the Michelin Man, seen so often in adverts at the time. It wrinkled, bulged and flapped around his white boots. With his splendid fireman's helmet, peaked at the front and back, hard, shiny and white, he looked as though he was off to a fancy dress party, rather than to fight fires in defence of the nation. Uniforms and helmets simply did not suit my academic husband's shambling white-haired persona.

Still, Malvern took his new duties seriously and for several weeks he went off to lectures and drills at the fire station. Then the great day arrived when the recruits were to fight their first fire. They set off with clanging bells and wailing sirens for the place where a magnificent blaze had been lit for the purpose, but on their way the clutch on the fire engine broke. They were left ignominiously sitting by the roadside waiting for another engine to come to the rescue. When it finally got them to the scene, all that was left were a few smouldering ashes. In the end, Malvern didn't see active service during his short spell as a fireman.

Chinks appearing

I was waiting in the wings of Port Elizabeth's Feather Market Hall, shaking with nerves, when a Black Sash colleague pulled me aside for a last word of advice: "Remember, Rosie, *apartheid* rhymes with *hate,* not *hide!*" This was not a last-minute indoctrination lesson. I needed no reminding that the system we were fighting was hate-filled and I had never been one for hiding, even when quaking in my boots. I was due to chair a public meeting to be addressed by Frederik van Zyl Slabbert, and my colleague's words were just a quick reminder to my stubbornly English tongue.

It was 1987 and something had happened that made us hopeful that there might at last be chinks in the state's armour. The Institute for a Democratic Alternative in South Africa (IDASA) had organised a conference in Dakar between a delegation of South Africans from within the country and another from the ANC in exile. On their return, delegates were aglow with stories of openness and conciliation. The banned and demonised ANC had been given a human face. The mutual willingness of the two parties to reach beyond the usual South African constraints was what grabbed the imagination.

The Dakar conference was followed by a series of reportbacks around the country. In Port Elizabeth, 1 600 people packed the Feather Market Hall to hear Van Zyl Slabbert speak. The hall was thundering with noise as toyi-toying and banner-wielding groups arrived and took their places, amid the visible presence of several "heavies" from a private security firm. There had been bomb threats and rumours that the meeting would be disrupted and I was disconcerted to see even the national co-ordinator of IDASA with a gun bulging out of his belt. As the meeting was co-sponsored by the Black Sash, I was chairing it, and while waiting in the wings I was reassured to see how nervous Van Zyl Slabbert was too!

His message was clear: if the political will was there, negotiation was still possible. If not, the alternative would be destruction. As the audience broke into shouts of "We are the future!" and "Slabbert! Slabbert!" I was amazed to see what reservoirs of hope and exuberance were released when people encountered signs of change. After the meeting we watched busloads of singing and chanting people drive off to the townships, followed closely by a phalanx of police vans. In the midst of this joyous scene I overheard a tight-lipped bystander remark, "And they expect us to treat them like human beings!" I was not surprised by the comment but nevertheless saddened that the uplifting evening should end on such a sour note.

In April 1989 my own chance came to meet the ANC in exile. I was invited to an IDASA conference in Harare, Zimbabwe, entitled "Women in the Struggle for Peace". Eighty South African women met at the conference, 55 were in the IDASA party and 25 were exiles from ANC missions around the world. This was an undreamt-of privilege and there was great excitement in our delegation, but also considerable anxiety. How would we all get on? Would there be police plants among us? Would we even be allowed to get there? I realised just how jittery some were when the woman who sat next to me on the plane clutched my arm and asked fearfully, "What's happening?" when the cabin lights went off for landing.

For me the overriding emotion was elation, and in that mood I fell in love with Harare. The broad streets and flowering trees, and the modest scale of the cathedral and law courts appealed to me. In so many colonies the architectural language was one of domination, with vast government structures dwarfing the buildings around, but in Harare it seemed to me the state buildings were perfectly proportioned. Each morning I got up early to pound the streets, relishing, as I walked, a sense of freedom from daily concerns and even from the chance of being followed or watched. The streets were clean and well kept and I was amazed at the size of some of the suburban properties, no doubt still tended by legions of servants. Cars seemed to be at a premium and I don't think I saw a single smart one. On one occasion a group of us hired a taxi that appeared to be held together by string – we had to hold onto the door to prevent it falling off! During a lunch break, a few of us were taken shopping by a member of the ANC delegation whose husband was the head of the organisation's mission in Harare. At one point her battered little car cut rather recklessly in front of another, and the obscenities yelled from that car window by its young white occupants were horrific. Our chaperone ignored the incident. "Don't worry," she said. "Be above it. We call them Rhodies; they aren't Zimbabweans."

The women in the IDASA delegation formed a disparate group, including community workers, journalists, doctors, lawyers, social workers, nursing sisters and housewives, all from a wide spectrum of political persuasions. There was a feisty academic from UWC ("University of the Wild Coloureds", she called it); a mother of an awaiting-trial prisoner on a treason charge; a cabaret artist whose songs brought tears to our eyes and who would later become an ANC MP; and a Democratic Party enthusiast who rather crassly urged everyone to vote DP, when many in her audience did not even have the vote. We were a mixed bunch indeed and judging by the conversation of some of the delegates, the Black Sashers sometimes felt way out on the far left wing.

The ANC women came as a surprise. We had known that they would be politically sophisticated, and the firebrands were certainly present. Some were young, glamorous and fashionably dressed, and highly articulate. They had been to the ANC school in Tanzania or to universities in the Eastern bloc or the States. The white women among them seemed to me to have a sneering tone, looking down on us as naïve, middle-class *amalungu* who came nowhere near matching their commitment to the cause. But most of us were surprised to find older women of enormous warmth and generosity, including three members of the ANC hierarchy. Many of them had been in exile for a very long time, some having left behind small children whom they would next meet as teenagers or adults. There was a grandmotherly communist with her East European accent and her braided hair, who defended Stalin with tears coursing down her cheeks; an erudite cultural attaché, graduate of Rutgers University, in jangling earrings and bracelets; and a razor-sharp barrister from London in a colourful, flowing sari.

It was apparent that the ANC women had planned very carefully for the conference and were strategic in their arguments and responses. By contrast, our group was too disparate for any cohesive thinking. As there were several of us from the Black Sash, we were at least able to caucus and present a united front. There were times of empty rhetoric and gross overstatement, when we seemed merely a gathering of Lenin's "useful idiots", and I wondered whether the whole conference was really just an ANC public relations exercise. At other times the divisions between the delegations seemed just too deep to cross. Discussions on conflict and violence threatened to degenerate into bitter recrimination, while thorny issues such as sanctions, majority rule, affirmative action and the economy gave rise to sharp differences too. Even the final plenary session was in danger of ending inconclusively, until Frene Ginwala, the barrister from London who would later become the first Speaker of the National Parliament, pulled together the many loose strands and highlighted our unity of purpose.

Several Zimbabwean women addressed the conference with lessons from their liberation experience. They lauded the vision of the gathering, regretting that Zimbabweans had not had a similar chance to meet and discuss their situation. Too many Rhodesians had tried to prevent the future instead of preparing for it. They pointed out that although Zimbabwean women had made major contributions to the liberation struggle, few received any political rewards. Many a story was told of how Comrade Freedom, who had fought alongside the men and commanded units during the war, had been relegated to tea girl during peacetime. "National liberation does not necessarily square up with female liberation," we were warned. Years later, reading about Mugabe's infamous Matabeleland massacres in

Peter Godwin's book *Mukiwa*, I did also wonder why events like that were airbrushed out of the conference.

In the documentary, *Chain of Tears*, directed by Toni Strasburg, we saw the effects on children of covert raids by the South African Defence Force, aimed at destabilising and flushing out opposition forces in Mozambique, Botswana and Angola. The full personal horror of it came home to us when we heard stories about some of the bombings suffered by those in exile. A young woman told of how her student husband was killed by a car bomb in Gaborone. She was late for work and he went outside to start the car. She heard a bang and a neighbour came running to tell her what had happened. "It is hard to tell what I saw," said Jackie through her tears. "Just pieces of his body." A young girl from Grahamstown who had fled the country at the time of the upheavals in the schools, wept one night as she told Ina Roux, a therapist and keen member of the Sash in Grahamstown and me, about her living conditions in exile, first in an ANC camp and then in Lusaka. She had left Grahamstown in a blaze of adventure but the reality of exile proved far from romantic. She earned 14 qwashas a month, plus a housing subsidy and food rations; 12 qwashas paid for a beer. The official word was that in Lusaka everyone was paid the same, from the leaders down to the lowliest messenger. Presumably exiles living in first-world cities enjoyed a much better lifestyle.

On the whole we were all careful not to fracture the conference's fragile unity, and sincere efforts were made to find ways of acknowledging a shared, if unequal, experience of oppression. The message that came through most clearly from all the ANC women was their longing to come home and be full human beings in the country of their birth. In summing up the conference, Frene Ginwala stressed that a chink had been opened in the barriers between us and that our mutual understanding had been enhanced through the exchange of personal experiences. In the end there was hardly a dry eye in the hall when we linked arms and sang *We Shall Overcome* and

Nkosi Sikelel' iAfrika. Even in spite of some troubling signs, there seemed to be so much hope for a bright future.

In January 1990, less than a year after Harare, a Cape Town colleague and I were invited to represent the Black Sash at another conference, this time in Amsterdam, which would again bring together delegations from inside South Africa and out. Organised by the Women's Committee of the Dutch Anti-Apartheid Movement, the Malibongwe conference, aimed to highlight the women's struggle. More than 150 South African women met to consider their role in the liberation movement and in a free and democratic South African future. FW de Klerk had just taken over from PW Botha as State President and of course he had earth-shaking surprises up his sleeve. But at least to us in the home delegation, his imminent announcement of the unbanning of the ANC was entirely unknown. Who knows how much the exile delegates knew?

We were due to fly to Amsterdam on New Year's Eve. Just after Christmas, Malvern, Charlotte, Lucy and I went to Nature's Valley for a few days of relaxation by the lagoon, meals out of doors and convivial conversations with friends. The forests encircling the valley were cool in the summer heat, and in the sea we spotted schools of dolphins. It was with some reluctance that I packed my suitcase with winter clothes and headed for the airport. Did I really want to be in Europe in January? My hesitation only increased when we got to the Port Elizabeth airport to find the concourse deserted and my name not on the passenger list. Time ticked by and the flight was about to be called when there was a sudden outbreak of hooting and screeching of brakes. A fleet of taxis disgorged the Port Elizabeth delegates and their supporters into the departures hall, several of them wearing the banned ANC colours and one of them waving our air tickets. "Grab your ticket!" shouted Malvern as I was swept up in the crowd, through the check-in gates and onto the plane without saying a proper goodbye. Lucy told me later how thrilling she'd found it to be surrounded by that crowd, feeling that the hopes and fears of South Africa went with our plane.

It was clear from the start that Malibongwe would be very different from the meeting in Harare. I soon realised that there were hidden agendas and complex intrigues that I in my naïve idealism had not anticipated. This time I was also more outspoken, and my criticisms did not go unmarked. "Are you for or against the ANC, Rosie?" a bemused Ruth Mpathi, one of the leaders of the ANC Women's League in exile would ask at the end. In Harare the ANC had addressed itself in fairly careful tones to the largely white contingent from South Africa. At Malibongwe the tone was different. The 150 women who travelled from South Africa came mostly from backgrounds of cruel and ongoing suffering and struggle, while those in exile in Africa, Europe and America seemed, by comparison, to be viewing the country through somewhat distant and analytical eyes. Karin Chubb, a fellow Sasher from Cape Town and I found the predominant focus on militarism and armed resistance quite disturbing. After hearing addresses by women from the Philippines struggle and the Cuban Women's Movement, and a female Palestinian soldier, we felt it would have been good to hear from women who had resisted oppression in non-violent ways, such as Argentinians or Indians. I became friendly with a young girl in our delegation who did development work in a small fishing community on the west coast of South Africa, where sand, sea and sky made up her horizon. She told me in horrified tones that two people at the conference were actively trying to recruit her for Umkhonto we Sizwe (MK), the armed wing of the ANC. Becoming a soldier was the last thing on her mind.

As with the Harare conference, the most important thing to come out of Malibongwe was the human contact, and this began even on the journey to Amsterdam. What should have been an overnight flight turned into a three-day excursion when our plane was diverted from a fog-engulfed Paris, to Toulouse and then Lyons. Travellers on South African passports were not allowed out of the transit lounge, which gave us plenty of time for bonding. I still had a British passport and had the added bonus of being able to make myself understood in French, thus

I soon became the chief negotiator with airline representatives, airport officials and police. I was just beginning to enjoy myself when my enthusiasm was firmly reined in by one of our party, a born again radical with the immortal words, "Rosemary, before you do anything further we must workshop this!" My family was delighted with this story and the phrase passed indelibly into Smith family parlance, to be used to subdue me whenever I became over-enthusiastic.

In the course of the long journey people began to swap life stories. I met the widow of one of the Cradock Four, Sicelo Mhlauli, who was a classmate of Lucy's at UCT. I made the acquaintance of Thandi Modise, the "knitting needles guerrilla", an MK operative whose cover was to carry a handbag with protruding knitting needles. Her two children had been brought up by her mother while she was in training camps in Botswana, Tanzania and Angola. As in Harare, I again met women who had forfeited their mothering for exile and the fight for liberation. It's a sacrifice I wholeheartedly respected, but not one I felt I could have made.

Amsterdam was grey and cold, brightened, thankfully, by the group of Dutch women who greeted us at the airport bearing bunches of flowers. And yet, just as I had begun to think that I was a South African after all, I fell in love with Europe all over again. I loved the tall, narrow houses, the bridges, canals and fleets of bicycles, and when darkness fell, the lighted windows revealing warm interiors which beckoned, often with Christmas trees still on show. One evening all the delegates had supper on board barges on the canals, before taking part in a torchlight procession accompanied by a jazz band and led by police on horseback. At night Karin and I would go to the American hotel adjacent to the conference centre and drink gluwein at midnight. It was great to be in a city again, and we felt enveloped in warm Dutch hospitality.

On our first day in Amsterdam we attended an ecumenical service entitled "Children and Peace" in the Dominicuskerk. Brass chandeliers lit the soaring ceiling and windows of the old church, and part of the service involved the lighting of candles.

It was an afternoon of juxtapositions as the warmth and light inside the church held back the icy darkness outside, and the melodic harmonies of singing contrasted with the harrowing stories told by South African women from the pulpit. It was a powerful start to our time together. Later that week, sitting in the Amsterdam City Hall, gilt mirrors sparkling, redolent of the grandeur of a golden age, I again had to pinch myself. Was I really sitting in Europe, amongst women from the ANC?

The first week was spent visiting small towns and meeting various women's and civil rights organisations, which had given money towards the conference. My party visited the city of Heerlen, two hours by train from Amsterdam. There, we spoke about ourselves and the organisations we represented. It was clear that most people thought of the South African struggle as a purely black one, so it gave me pleasure to talk about the work of the Black Sash. At the end of the day we were each given an album with photos and messages. One of the messages said, "Dear Rosemary. For me it was very surprising to see a white woman who fights active against apartheid."

One day we saw the film of André Brink's novel, *A Dry White Season*. Portraying detention and police brutality on township streets, the film had been banned in South Africa. Except for a fine performance by Marlon Brando, it was not a great artistic achievement, but its impact on the audience of Malibongwe delegates affected me deeply. For many it was a painful experience seeing a mirror of their own tragedies on screen. Women began to keen and some had to leave the cinema. I had never experienced such identification with a film and I was extremely moved.

I made friends with fellow delegates and began to feel at home in the Malibongwe milieu. But once the closed sessions commenced and we began to tackle issues in smaller groups, the mood changed. The ANC delegates now seemed harder and I sensed that it became necessary for them to toe the party line. There was little genuine exploration of world-views or searching analysis of power structures. Dissension was not easily brooked, but Karin and I were impressed by a woman who worked for the ANC in East Germany. She was open in her disillusionment with communism and the ANC. Exile, for her, had become a bitter experience. Karin visited her in Berlin afterwards and said that she was wondering where her place in the new South Africa would be.

For myself there were moments when I felt distinctly uncomfortable. During the debate on the End Conscription Campaign (ECC), for instance, it became clear that the ANC viewed the ECC as an offshoot of their armed struggle. I knew from experience that many embraced the ECC as a pacifist cause, and when I said so, I could sense the general antagonism. In a plenary discussion on Palestine and Israel, Karin and I dissented in the face of the overwhelming consensus in favour of Palestine. There were many Jewish members in the Black Sash who would have rejected the conference's simplistic analysis of the Middle East situation, and we felt compelled to represent them. Swimming against the tide gave us a slithery sensation of fear. It was small wonder that Ruth Mpati questioned my allegiance as she said goodbye to me at Schipol airport. I felt I had to digest all that I had seen and heard and so my response was simply to shrug and smile.

The conference had culminated in a series of discussions on women's unity, and as the delegations parted and went their separate ways – some home to South Africa, others not – we were all aware that much remained to be done to ensure the fair representation of women in the new South Africa.

Airport authorities at Schipol were lenient about overweight baggage for our return flight. Several women had acquired large bags, which they had filled with winter coats, boots and other goodies that had been on offer to delegates who were not equipped for the severe Dutch winter. At Jan Smuts airport, where overweight restrictions on domestic flights were much more stringent, these bulging bags caused great consternation, with racist accusations beginning to fly in all directions. The situation was exacerbated when one of the Port Elizabeth delegates was marched off to a customs office. At the end of the conference we had been told emphatically to destroy any literature that might be banned in South Africa, but as it turned out, that was not this woman's sin. The offending item was a small rubber doll, complete with urinating penis!

Shortly after our return home, FW de Klerk made his momentous announcement. The ANC was to be unbanned and Nelson Mandela released. The news exceeded our wildest dreams. Was the struggle won? Were we about to see the dawning of non-racialism and equal opportunity, service delivery, an end to poverty, education for all, a new constitution, open media and freedom of speech? Would this country at last be able to hold its head high? The euphoria was almost unbearable; I wanted to dance in the streets. Of course there were dangers ahead and much to be negotiated, the quagmire of political jostling not the least of it; but the world was right to hail this as a miracle nation and I was proud to be part of it.

Improvements in progress

"It is a hot day in the Western Cape," the TV commentator noted uninspiringly. Unused to momentous moments such as this, he grew increasingly banal as the waiting dragged on. "The sun beats down relentlessly in Africa," he tried again. The camera continued to stare at the gates of the Victor Verster prison in Paarl. It was 11 February 1990, the day of Nelson Mandela's release after 27 years in jail. Malvern and I sat fixed to the television awaiting a glimpse of the man whose name we knew so well but whose banned image had hardly ever been seen in South Africa. At last the waiting crowd exploded with excitement and there he was, hand in hand with Winnie, acknowledging the roaring greeting. I felt a lump in my throat. A few months previously in Amsterdam such an event had not seemed possible. We watched every move of the cavalcade as it made its way to the Grand Parade in Cape Town where the icon of the struggle was to make his first public address. There, from a balcony overlooking the jubilant crowd, Mandela took my breath away when he publicly thanked two white organisations for their contribution to the liberation struggle: the National Union of South African Students (NUSAS) and the Black Sash. It was an unexpected and unbelievable moment.

Lucy, a UCT student at the time, was in the crowd on the Grand Parade. She and her group of friends were ecstatic, but they decided to move off when some breaking of shop windows and hasty looting began nearby. It was inevitable that opportunists would seize the moment, and in their rash act they provided a warning of the roller-coaster ride that lay ahead. The ANC colours started to appear everywhere, on cup, scarf, shirt and cap, and the South African Communist Party flag was flown openly. Euphoria and hope were in the air, as was an exciting feeling of comradeship among all those who had taken part in struggle-related activities. We really seemed to be entering a wonderful non-racial period. The Black Sash national conference was held in Grahamstown that year, and while joy and elation were present there too, I was impressed by the clear-headed realism that marked the discussions. With its hard-won experience of the dynamics that had been brewing in the country, especially through the 1980s, the Black Sash knew that some very delicate and perilous work awaited all South Africans. Much thought was given to the new role the organisation would have to play in a radically altered socio-political landscape.

At this time the Jan Smuts air terminal in Johannesburg was undergoing renovations. Notices were put up depicting a cartoon figure losing his balance on a slippery floor. "Improvements in Progress!" the signs warned. As the year unfolded, change and improvement did indeed seem like a slippery floor to me, and that image became more and more apt. Bronwyn Brady, our young fieldworker at the time, was rushed off her feet as the Sash participated in ever more meetings and rallies and joined in the general bustling among comrades. Soon, however, we all found ourselves longing for less rhetoric and strategy, and more in-depth consideration of policies. As shared jubilation gave way to a rising sweep of triumphalism, we became concerned to see the rallies turn more and more militant. Amid the inevitable jostling and competition among factions, we were sometimes caught awkwardly in the middle. We soon realised that we would have to cling firmly to our independence. In the words of the Black Sash dedication, we were pledged to "uphold the ideals of mutual trust and forbearance, of sanctity of word, of courage for the future and of peace and justice for all persons and peoples." At a time when national values were up for renegotiation, we steadfastly had to resist any diminution of these principles.

As our Zimbabwean sisters in Harare had warned, once the struggle was over the role of Comrade Freedom would be at severe risk if we did not guard it carefully. Many women in Zimbabwe felt that they'd been sidelined to the cooking pots after the war. I was reminded of this when plans were being made for a massive rally in the Bisho stadium at which Mandela would be present and the Black Sash in East London were asked to do the catering. The request gave rise to heated debate. We certainly needed to reassess our role in the activist arena, but should a human rights organisation be relegated to the task of catering? On this occasion the East Londoners decided to join in the spirit of the hour and do the task assigned to them, but we all undertook to remain vigilant in this regard.

All roads led to Bisho on that memorable day. Every form of transport had been commandeered and taxis and vans were bursting with people. The white section of neighbouring King William's Town was cordoned off, in fear and trepidation of the black invasion. A small group from the Grahamstown Sash found a spot to perch on some rising ground overlooking the vast crowd. People stood shoulder to shoulder, helicopters hovered overhead. Marshals were searching everyone who entered the stadium, confiscating any sharp objects which could lead to trouble. At last Mandela arrived in a high-speed convoy of cars, some with blackened windows. From where we stood we could see only a vague outline of the man, but it was the roar of the crowd and the soaring singing that made the day most memorable.

I had to wait two years to have more than just a distant glimpse of Nelson Mandela. In November 1992 I was invited to a lunch in his honour in the Albany Recreation Centre, hosted by the Grahamstown Civic Organisation (GRACO). This was the hall where Malvern and I had attended a service many years earlier when Allan Hendrickse had been detained. It was on that Sunday, twenty years before, that I had decided to start keeping a diary. In the interim I had been to many meetings in that hall, some of them secret, some more overt. To see Nelson Mandela there felt like a circle completed.

GRACO was an organisation run by coloured Grahamstonians and the Recreation Hall was in the coloured area. After the lunch Mandela was due to attend a rally at a stadium in the black township. I was intrigued by this order of events. Was it a shrewd political move by the ANC to garner coloured support? Or had the coloured community stolen a march on the township? In any event, it was a wonderful occasion. The usually bare hall was transformed with flowers and balloons and a large welcoming banner hung above the stage. We sat at trestle tables groaning under platters of food, which ranged from curry and legs of lamb to trifle and mousse. A centrepiece of fruit gave the occasion the air of a banquet. Outside the hall a crowd gathered, and we knew when Mandela had arrived from the customary roar that greeted him. A red carpet stretched from pavement to hall and two little girls dressed in white held flower baskets full of corsages, which they presented to the VIPs. One of the girls was called Zinzi, the same name as one of Mandela's daughters, and later he had a photograph taken of her sitting on his knee. I recalled reading an interview with him in which he said that the absence of children during his prison years had been one of his most severe deprivations.

Inside the hall there were presentations of gifts, speeches of welcome and toasts. As I looked about, I mused on past occasions in that hall and on my fellow guests. There were people I had worked with at GADRA and in many other non-governmental organisations. I was one of only a handful of whites. I felt deeply privileged and knew that it was thanks to the Black Sash that I was there. Alongside me sat a well-known Grahamstown couple, he a Black Consciousness priest who had spent time on Robben Island and she an acerbic academic. They'd always had a way of deflating my naïve enthusiasms and even on this occasion they seemed mocking of my excitement. "So, Rosemary, aren't you feeling important, being here today."

But nothing could destroy the magic for me. Mandela looked younger than I had imagined, a man of charisma and strength, and as he spoke I thought, "Here is a person really in touch with himself." He spoke for 45 minutes without a note, in humble vein and on the theme of reconciliation. He recollected that the first coloured people he had met had been members of the Garment Workers' Union, women who had impressed him with their strength and ferocity. He told of arguments in prison with Neville Alexander, a coloured leader and educationalist who had urged that in a new South Africa, Afrikaans should be abolished for having been the language of the oppressor. He spoke of various prison warders who had shown him kindness. I heard Mandela speak again on various occasions afterwards and saw him at other functions in Grahamstown, but nothing could eclipse that first time in the Recreation Hall.

A new dawn had broken but it was clear the path, finally visible ahead, would be long. First of all, preparations for the election had to be made. But at the same time, the shape of the future had to be negotiated. Not only did first generation civil and political rights have to be secured, but it was also up to organisations such as ours to ensure that the second and third generation rights like social security, education, adequate wages, peace, a healthy environment and opportunities for development were not left out of the blueprint.

The immediate challenge, in Grahamstown as elsewhere, was the establishment of transitional local government structures in which both the expertise of the old civic structures and the political aspirations of the new guard were accommodated. This was often an unequal and acrimonious tussle as the community-based organisations tended to be poorly equipped and easily duped, while the established authorities were in a state of disorganised retreat, unsure of their future and sensing the carpet gradually being pulled from under their feet. In these scenarios the Black Sash played a consulting role. Our fieldworker Glenn Hollands was now a highly skilled negotiator who had earned widespread credibility in the Grahamstown community, and most of this delicate work fell to him. Glenn's top priority was that a climate of free political participation be maintained.

In preparation for the transition that lay ahead, we renewed what we had in the past called "white outreach", a range of projects aimed at white Grahamstonians. Sociologists, when they describe a country's development, talk of societies as either "ascribing" or "achieving". An ascribing society clings to the past and to values handed down by previous generations, making it difficult to adjust to changes in the outside world. In an achieving society people are no longer imprisoned by the past but look outward with confidence towards the future. The transition can be painful, as people have to abandon certainties that had previously given shape to their lives. It was this process of adaptation that we were anticipating when we launched a series of public panel discussions entitled, "Signposts to the New South Africa". We had a range of good speakers and interesting topics, but the audiences were sparse and the impact probably did not warrant the amount of work we put in. We managed to reach a larger audience at the National Arts Festival in 1992, when I was asked to be part of a panel discussion entitled "Living Space for All", which addressed the future of town planning.

I found myself on a platform with some leading South African architects and an ANC spokesperson on housing. My humble brief was to describe housing conditions in Grahamstown and I was glad of the opportunity, hoping that somewhere someone of influence might be listening. I invited the audience to look out from the large plate-glass windows of the monument, over the town to the township, and to observe the hillside peppered with wattle and daub houses. Erected by the people themselves of tree poles and mud, these primitive structures had proliferated since 1989 when restrictions were being loosened and spontaneous land invasions had begun on every available patch of vacant land in and around the township. The last time any official housing development had occurred had been in the 1960s, and by the 1980s the situation had become dire.

In the townships up to 150 people shared a standing water pipe per street. Just a few months before the 1992 festival some of the taps had had to be closed because of the drought, but at the same time the city council decided to cut bulk electricity and water supplies to the township because of outstanding debts. February in Grahamstown is suffocatingly hot and that year was no exception. In the township there was an appalling stench as sewage was not being washed away. A range of local organisations appealed against the council's inhumane action but to no avail. Tensions rose as residents were forced to carry water from the town and before long the security forces, still controlled by the Nationalist government, began to prepare for the inevitable backlash.

Late one afternoon, when rumours of stoning and police harassment began to drift into the Black Sash office, Glenn and I decided to drive to the township. On the way we passed a police roadblock, where we discussed the situation with the officer in charge. In the township we met with leaders of the civic organisations and together we decided to appeal for road tankers to ferry water. When we left the house where we had met, everything seemed quiet. There did not appear to be anyone in the streets and we decided to return to town by a different route. At one point we noticed a young boy standing on a bank overlooking the road, and when the first small stone hit the car we thought it was youthful mischief. But as we rounded the bend it was immediately clear that this was no child's play. There were knots of people waiting along the road ahead, all with stones in hand. By this stage it was impossible to turn around and all Glenn could do was put his foot down.

When the first missile came through the window we realised that we were being pelted with bricks. I ducked down, but not before I was hit on the side and showered with glass from the shattering windscreen. The sound of bricks thumping and windows splintering was all I could hear. "This is what war is like," I thought. I was frightened and certain we were going to die. From my crouched position I could not see the raised fists and the looks of hatred on people's faces, but those were the images Glenn registered as he drove furiously down the road. The police at the roadblock wanted to take us to the hospital, but we declined their help and went to the doctor ourselves. Amazingly, Glenn had only a small scratch, but the car was extensively damaged and I was severely bruised down one side, with glass in my hair and several cuts on my head. All the doctor could do was administer anti-tetanus injections and bathe some of the worst cuts. I had to go home and slowly remove all the glass in a bath.

I was shocked, but also deeply saddened that the divisions in our society seemed to be widening rather than closing. The images in my mind that night were not just of flying bricks and shattering glass. There was also one of a mother and her small child sitting in the doctor's waiting room as we stumbled in. The mother was horrified at what she saw and hid her child's face in her lap. "Did kaffirs do this to you?" she asked. Glenn must have been even more haunted than I was, but he never mentioned it. I think the event was eclipsed for him a while later when he again found himself on a battlefield, only this time with real bullets whizzing around his head. He attended a protest march in Bisho where the Ciskei police opened fire, killing several people and wounding others. For Glenn, that was far more frightening.

As for me, I asked my friend and GADRA colleague Kholeka Nkwinti to take me in her car the very next day, along the road where the stoning had happened, so that I could exorcise my fear. Nevertheless, it was some time before the incident faded and even the sound of acorns raining down on the roof of my car could bring back terrifying memories.

We learnt later that several other vehicles were stoned that day and that a pedestrian was killed by a swerving car. The elderly couple inside were critically injured when the driver lost control. The one bit of good news was that the essential services were restored to the townships the next day. When word got out that workers from the Black Sash had been stoned, we received many phone calls of regret and condolence from township residents. A letter appeared in the local paper deploring the violence. While not condoning it, we realised that this was sometimes the only way people could find to express their frustration. We had been in the wrong place at the wrong time.

The day after the stoning, a few of us drove to Cradock. The Minister of Health and Welfare was visiting the town and we decided to challenge her with some pertinent questions on proposed amendments to the Social Assistance Bill, which would affect social pensioners. The Black Sash had been targeting members of both the Nationalist cabinet and the opposition with questions on welfare issues, and we could not let this opportunity go by. The Black Sash vehicle wasn't in a fit state to be driven and I wasn't much better, but we went in a colleague's car and I spent the three-hour journey lying on the back seat nursing my bruises.

The meeting in the Cradock Town Hall was a typical small-town occasion. The respectful audience was dressed as though for church, and at the end of the minister's speech she was presented with a pot of homemade jam. In spite of clearly being outsiders we dominated question time, firing our salvos from the back of the hall. The minister did not ignore us, continued talking to us at teatime, and a week later there arrived a salmon pink, gold-embossed card with the assurance that she had heard our cries. I don't know how much our particular efforts helped, but in due course some significant concessions were made, allowing the Black Sash to feel rewarded for its relentless campaign on social pensions. The points gained were that women would henceforth qualify for old-age pensions at 60; that "foreigners" would not include homeland citizens; and that the words "at the Minister's discretion" would be altered to indicate that pensions were a right and not a privilege.

Over tea and koeksisters that day we also encountered the glamorous Martha Olckers, one-time Mayor of Grahamstown, who had since carved out a career for herself in national politics. In conversation with her, we challenged her on the callous Nationalist legacy that still led to incidents like the Grahamstown water cuts. Martha maintained her glossy composure, deigning only to say how pleased she was that there had been no violence – upon which my companions had to restrain me from tearing open my dress and displaying a bright purple bosom!

As South Africa inched its way towards its first democratic election amidst increasing violence, Charles Dickens' famous line from *A Tale of Two Cities* had never seemed more apt to me – it was indeed the best and the worst of times. According to the South African Institute of Race Relations, in 1993 alone, 3 706 people died in political violence. When Chris Hani, ex-commander of MK and a popular ANC leader, was assassinated in April of that year, an outpouring of emotional outrage followed, with violence directed at any institution vaguely representing the state. Covert, so-called third-force operations by the far right stoked up tensions between warring parties, resulting in high levels of black-on-black violence. Meanwhile the PAC continued the armed struggle with attacks on soft targets. A prominent incident was the murder of white American student Amy Biehl, by PAC youths in Guguletu, Cape Town.

Across the country, members of the Black Sash served on peace committees and monitoring groups. Although the situation in the Eastern Cape never became as explosive as it was in Natal and on the Reef, our region too had need of its peace monitors. It was difficult to evaluate their true impact, but their distinctive blue bibs, emblazoned with the symbol of a dove, were widely seen as a reassuring and restraining presence at marches and meetings, which even in the ANC heartland sometimes turned confrontational.

In Natal, where the Inkatha Freedom Party (IFP) and the ANC were desperately manoeuvring for power, the conflict was at times nothing short of an all-out war. We were mindful of this on the night a few of us decided to attend a glamorous costume party. The Grand Victorian Ball was to be held in the City Hall to commemorate Dick King's epic journey on horseback from Port Natal 150 years before, carrying a despatch from the war that was then raging. The idea of a ball was enticing and we decided to enjoy a fling. The costumes were half the fun, with farmers' wives appearing in their ancestors' ball gowns and Malvern in his top hat looking like the March Hare from *Alice in Wonderland*. A red carpet stretched from pavement to hall, lined with boys in scarlet cadet band uniforms and leopard skin drapes, holding blazing torches. On the printed programme was a quote from Mrs Beeton's *Manners of Polite Society*, warning, "If a lady waltz with you, beware not to press her waist. Only lightly touch it with the palm of your hand, lest you leave a disagreeable impression not only on her dress, but also on her mind." It was the last gasp of colonialism and the past, and we danced all night.

In the months preceding the election, Black Sash branches throughout the country engaged in a campaign to educate first-time voters. Our region was predominantly rural and our team of 15 Sash members, which included an indefatigable septuagenarian, travelled enormous distances. We concentrated mostly on large, well-mechanised pineapple and chicory farms, dairy farmlands and industrialised citrus co-operatives, but also visited parts of the drought-ridden hinterland where often the general farming infrastructure was extremely run-down. The venues for our workshops included barns and cowsheds, and once a hotel. Often people sat on bales of hay in dim light from paraffin lamps. In an area of 3 000 square kilometres, we travelled 6 000 kilometres to reach an estimated 4 200 farm workers.

On the whole, white farmers were uncompromising about the privacy of their land and exerted strict control over access to those who lived there. A generally conservative community, they had also come to regard the Black Sash with suspicion and even hostility, owing in part to our collaboration with an NGO called the East Cape Agricultural and Rural Project (ECARP), which had offices above us in Bathurst Street. We had to promote the voter education project with great care in order not to alarm the farmers. We spoke at agricultural meetings, met with individual farmers and wrote articles for the press, and in general were positively received. Often a farmer would co-ordinate the workshop arrangements for us, even transporting workers from surrounding farms.

Glenn wrote a play called *Balloting Blues*, complete with a rap song, which was performed in isiXhosa at our workshops. The play dramatised the choices facing a first-time voter, emphasising the point that his or her vote was their secret. Empowered by this knowledge, our protagonist, Nosipho, a domestic worker, was able to navigate her way through various forms of pressure and intimidation from her husband, her community and her employer. After the play, a mock ballot was held so that people could practise voting. Young and old, women and men, they came in their hundreds to watch the play and cast their first "vote".

Because we were reaching out to workers, these educational sessions had to take place either at night or on Saturdays. I discovered places in the Eastern Cape that I had never seen before, tucked away and reached only on rough roads, up steep rocky valleys and over dry riverbeds. We got used to natural history excursions as the car headlights picked out buck, rabbits, mice and other small mammals crossing the rural roads. One night a large hare got trapped in our headlights and raced ahead of the car for a long stretch of gravel road. There were potholes and dongas and roads sloping off into the veld, and many times the team got lost in the profound darkness.

One farm, which we visited on a bright Saturday morning, seemed like the original Garden of Eden, with flowering hedges in profusion along the roadside. But we soon discovered it was far from paradise. The workers lived in wattle and daub houses and had no toilets; the school had broken windows and badly fitting doors; and we discovered that the farmer had instructed his labourers whom they were to vote for. Some empowering education was clearly needed. At other times, though, we encountered people who knew their own minds. "My party isn't on the ballot sheet!" one bent old woman complained as she emerged from the make-believe polling booth. It transpired that she wanted to vote for Umkhonto we Sizwe. One late afternoon we held an impromptu workshop at a road workers' camp, where we squashed into a tin hut with people sitting on benches while pots bubbled on a stove at the far end. It was an all-male audience and some of the faces looked weather-beaten and worn. As they cast their mock votes, I wondered how much life would really change for them in the new democracy.

There was a special pleasure for me in working with first-time voters, because I was at last to be one myself. In preparation for the election, the government expedited new applications for citizenship, and this time I had no doubt that the time was right for me to become a South African citizen. So it was that I was able to stand in one of the legendary queues on 27 April 1994 and step into a booth to finally place my first cross in a South African election.

The day dawned windy and dusty. Malvern manned a polling booth in the township, where the queues of first-time voters snaked out of school buildings and church halls. The Black Sash helped to staff the Independent Electoral Commission's monitoring centre, with its operations room in the offices of the Albany Council of Churches. Our job was to receive phone reports from monitors throughout the rural districts, and our chief operator was Nancy Charton, an Anglican priest and long-serving Sash member. Nancy stands out in my mind as a legendary figure who once stared down a military roadblock. On that distant Saturday morning in the mid-80s, a phalanx of security vehicles had blocked our access to Joza township, preventing us from attending a funeral. We were a motley crew of Sashers and students, and at our head was Nancy, grey hair whisping out from a bun, a battered straw hat on her head. Undaunted by the show of might in our path, Nancy mustered us into a circle in the road and proceeded to lead us in prayer. The young soldiers watched impassively, until the special branch drove up and gave us ten minutes to disperse. Now, years later, Nancy led our team of election monitors with that same ebullience, concluding her calls – to the astonishment of correspondents at the other end of the line – with her personal signature, "Receiving you loud and clear. Hallelujah!" As the day progressed, a berg wind began to rage. One of the messages from a small rural hamlet reported that the polling station, a tent, had blown away. To escape the dust, the reporter was phoning from inside a big plastic rubbish bag.

No one was surprised when the ANC gained a resounding victory. Come Inauguration Day on 10 May, we again had to pinch ourselves to make sure that this was real. Were we really seeing South African Defense Force generals saluting Mandela? Was that Fidel Castro on our television screens? And was this really all happening in Pretoria, seat of the Nationalist government for over 40 years?

Against the backdrop of Sir Herbert Baker's majestic Union Buildings, the inauguration was immensely joyous. Our friend and fellow Sasher, Mary-Louise Peires, attended the occasion as the spouse of an ANC MP and she sent us a colourful description. People were in best dress and hat, exotic robes and turbans. She carried her own hat in a paper bag for most of the day and was accosted at one point by another spouse of a newly elected MP who had got rather used to all the freebies they'd been receiving. She wanted to know where the hats were being handed out. During the fly-past of the air force jets Mary-Louise overheard someone remark, "Isn't it wonderful to think that those planes now belong to us."

There were still the obvious vestiges of colonialism, with the navy band playing *Land of Hope and Glory* and boys in striped blazers and flannels serving food in a marquee. But the overwhelming feeling, for the duration of that day at least, was that all South Africans were equal at last, bowed down no more by fear, despair, oppression or guilt. I felt content and happy to number myself as one of them.

Knitting with barbed wire

As we watched a rainbow of condensation from the air force jets drifting above the Union Buildings, it was tempting to believe that the miracle was complete. Many colleagues and friends did indeed believe that politically at least, their contribution was over. Those of us who were more involved in social work, however, knew that the struggle was far from finished. "Rainbow" and "miracle" were glib words to describe what had happened so far, but poverty was not going to be exorcised by an election victory; forgiveness and reconciliation were not going to be ushered in by glorious inauguration pageants. Tackling these challenges still lay ahead. I felt that I had energy for the task and looked forward to the final phase of my working life.

In 1995 the Black Sash met for its final national conference, to decide on its own dissolution. Our numbers had always been low, certainly relative to the amount of work we'd succeeded in doing, and lately they had shrunk even further. Some women were joining the newly unbanned organisations, some were feeling burnt out and wanted to do other things with their lives, and some felt the victory had been won. Our size had never daunted or embarrassed us. Indeed, the voice of a small group of dedicated women had had a penetrating effect in the call against white domination. But what credibility would such a voice have now, should it need to speak out against the failures or abuses of a majority government? In a free political environment communities were beginning to speak for themselves, and rather than cling to the past, the Sash decided to confront its own demise. Consultants were engaged for a strategic evaluation, and while the advice offices were considered indispensable, the work of the more politically inclined volunteer arm of the organisation was judged to have run its course. At the next conference the Black Sash as we knew it was disbanded. The network of advice offices was transformed into a professional non-governmental organisation overseen by the Black Sash Trust. Already the advice offices, which operated in four provinces, employed up to 50 people and operated on an annual budget of over R4 million.

It was an emotional moment when the curtain came down. We knew as we agreed to hang up our sashes that we were bidding farewell to something irreplaceable. We had been a tightly knit group, bound by a single and sacred purpose, who had trusted and respected each other implicitly. Even our social lives had become bound up in the association. In many ways the Sash had been my life. In it I had found my own identity and formed many of my closest bonds. The camaraderie had been a very fine experience for me, as had the depth of education I had received. In the three decades that I had by then lived in South Africa, no other organisation could have integrated me so meaningfully into the life of the country or taught me so much about it. Nevertheless I supported the decision to disband. My own involvement in the revamped advice office structure was set to continue, not only locally but also nationally through my continuing role in the Black Sash Trust.

Transforming a volunteer-driven organisation into an employee-based one proved more difficult than anticipated. At the same time funding started to dry up as foreign donors concluded that the fight for human rights had been won. It was at this critical time that I decided to accept a full-time post as manager of the advice office in Grahamstown. My social work with GADRA had always overlapped with my voluntary work for the Black Sash, so the change felt right. What I did not anticipate was how difficult it would be to manage colleagues who had previously operated as free agents, loosely overseen by a volunteer committee. At first we circled each other warily. The wise and unflappable Gus Macdonald, my friend from our days in Kansas, became the office secretary and was always on hand to tone down my fervour when necessary. But soon the challenges of our day-to-day work in a new socio-political context took our minds off ourselves and began to cement us.

Fortunately many erstwhile volunteers continued to support and assist the new professional organisation, enhancing our work and ensuring that skills were transferred to new staff. The area in which I most appreciated this support was the realm of finance, my Achilles heel. I remember sobbing quietly in the back row during maths exams at school. Numbers floored – and bored – me. When my exasperated teacher asked, "Rosemary, how are you going to look after your own money?" I airily replied, "I shall have an accountant." Of course life doesn't always dish up personal administrative assistants and my innumeracy haunted me throughout my working life. When it came to number crunching, the national director of the Sash described me as "a long-time Sasher but a loud teeth gnasher." Fortunately financial acumen was a skill that was well represented among Grahamstown members of the Black Sash and for years our meticulous bookkeepers watched my back.

My time as manager of the advice office was another rich period in my life as I formed close and interesting friendships with managers from across the country. They were all younger than me and we tended to keep very different hours at our workshops and conferences, but I enjoyed their dynamic conversation and they seemed to value my experience, also regarding me as a kind of agony aunt who would listen patiently to their romantic turmoils.

Transition from an unequal society was never going to be a seamless process and it was incumbent on previously privileged South Africans to facilitate the transfer in all spheres of society. Sadly, apartheid had stifled the education of the majority for so long that the task of bridging the gap was enormous. Furthermore, when the new dispensation arrived, the newcomers were impatient and the old hands felt threatened, often taking early retirement packages. It was a shortsighted policy and, as we saw in our dealings with new provincial departments, often disastrous for our clients. It was exciting to see some of our comrades from the struggle now besuited and sitting in high places, but as one of them confessed, many of them had turned into "Guavas": they were Going Up And Very Ambitious.

"Where to Now?" was the title of a meeting convened in 1995 by the Social Workers' Council in the Eastern Cape. For the first time in my experience, the meeting was dominated by social workers of colour who asked all the questions that were on our minds too. There weren't too many answers yet, but the landscape was definitely changing. The president and registrar, both still of the old guard, tried to respond with the same old tired social work phrases from an outdated era, but they were not allowed to get away with it. The mood of the meeting was captured in the vote of thanks, when the portly registrar was described as "very transparent" but also "very visible".

We truly were in a new world, and not an easy one for South Africans to adjust to. A friend once described untangling a clumsy piece of writing as "knitting with barbed wire". That was what it felt like in South Africa. So many of the welfare and developmental problems required Herculean interventions, but fraud and corruption bedevilled the scene. In November 1996 the *Daily Dispatch* reported one example: R2,5 million had been stolen from the Eastern Cape Central Health and Welfare Department, with seven officials dismissed for negligence.

In a rather vacuous but uncannily prescient statement, the Queen of England put her finger on it. "You must be so busy!" she said to everyone she greeted on her royal visit to this country in 1995. Addressing parliament in Cape Town she said, "Ever since my previous visit in 1947, I have wanted to return to this magnificent country. That wish has never deserted me through half a century in which you have seen turmoil and tragedy." She bestowed on Nelson Mandela an Honorary Order of Merit and referred to the new South Africa as little short of a miracle.

Part of her tour included a visit to Port Elizabeth and Malvern and I received an embossed invitation to take tea in the presence of Her Majesty. I was thrilled, privately pleased that Malvern and I were to be singled out in this way and always ready to enjoy some pageantry. The royal reception happened to clash with a regional meeting of advice office managers in Port Elizabeth, but I discovered that the manager of the Port Elizabeth office had also been invited, so the two of us broached the subject of having the afternoon off. Our colleagues had little patience with our enthusiasm for the British Queen. "What has she to do with the Sash?" they wanted to know. Nevertheless we won the day, and on a lovely March afternoon, Laura Best, Malvern and I entered the hallowed portals of the Port Elizabeth Club. Malvern and I were soberly dressed but Laura had on a long gown and squashy velvet hat she had acquired at the Grahamstown Festival. She was bent on having fun. A band played on the lawns of the club and out in the street an excited throng was waving flags. When the dignitaries arrived we were thrilled by the equerries' dazzling uniforms and by Port Elizabeth's handsome mayoral couple in full beaded Xhosa regalia.

The royal party had spent the morning visiting the Missionvale Care Centre in New Brighton, after which the chartered Rolls-Royce had broken down, hence the Queen's late arrival at the club. Dressed in turquoise, she seemed very small as she entered the room where we were lining the walls, ready with our smiles and curtsies. In fact, her handbag seemed to dwarf her. She promptly circulated, stopping to speak to whomever took her fancy, which sadly did not include the Sash representatives. She did speak to a Salvation Army officer standing near me and to a Rhodes University law professor, both of whom reported that her only comment had been, "You must be so busy."

And busy we were indeed. The Truth and Reconciliation process occupied our efforts and emotions for many months, and in 1998 SANGOCO, a coalition of South African non-governmental organisations, arranged a similar travelling campaign entitled "Speak Out on Poverty". Hearings were held around the country, enabling the poor to speak out in public about their plight. Among the commissioners was our own Black Sash national stalwart Sheena Duncan. We went to a lot of trouble organising the hearing in our local town hall, publicising the event extensively and attracting people from the rural hinterland. Even for us, who were well briefed about the situation in our province, the hearing was deeply moving and revealed new depths to the state of poverty in the Eastern Cape. It also underlined the confusions and difficulties resulting from the devolution of power to the provincial departments, as well as the frequent lack of concern on the part of officialdom. "The clerks always tell us that the problem is in Bisho," said one desperate woman. "We don't even know where Bisho is from here." "The officials are not interested," said another. "They are just throwing butter in our eyes."

As well as stories of dire destitution the commission also heard many of tenacious survival. People were engaging in small businesses, craft ventures, water projects. Somehow people were devising means to fend for themselves. Some had failed, but many were still full of courage and determination to try again, needing only some development assistance. Sadly, the poverty project came to naught. I still consider it a disgrace that there was no follow-up, after all the publicity and anticipation. The most we could hope for was that the relevant departments had taken note and that more development projects would be put in place. But we in the advice offices felt rather ashamed about the expectations that had been raised, never to be fulfilled.

Some of the barbed wire snares that entangled our clients were laid by unscrupulous insurance and loan agencies. Over time, our advice office built up considerable knowledge on insurance practices. Margaret Kenyon and Viv Botha, two members who made this their special area of expertise, found that people often mistook an insurance policy for a saving scheme, thus easily falling prey to silver-tongued agents. People were confused about surrender values and premium deductions, and had clutches of insurance policies which ate into their meagre salaries. We became like insurance brokers ourselves as we tried to explain the technical details of the policies, and we listened to endless stories of fraudulent practices. One man was paid out a large sum into his bank account, half of which was immediately withdrawn by his insurance agent who had tricked him into divulging his secret account number. Another sales representative persuaded a whole battalion of soldiers to sign stop orders for long-term insurance policies, leaving them with very little disposable income at the end of each month. Two years after taking out their policies, the soldiers wanted to know where their promised caravans were! Sometimes cases took so long to resolve that one woman compared her saga to a series of episodes from the soap opera *The Bold and the Beautiful*.

When we learnt that road workers were becoming easy targets for travelling agents, our interpreter and I headed to a place en route to East London euphemistically called "Lovers' Twist", where extensive roadworks were in progress. We talked along the roadside to men operating picks and shovels, and at lunchtime we spoke to them in the wooden shed, which operated as a canteen. "Taking out insurance is like buying a pair of shoes," we advised them. "If it pinches, don't purchase." Whenever possible we lobbied the insurance industry, urging that companies should be held responsible for the conduct of their agents.

As the network of advice offices linked into a national one, we were able to pick up common problems and build up dossiers to make the Sash voice stronger. Insurance matters became our speciality in Grahamstown and we produced an easy-to-understand booklet providing guidance on insurance practices. The Knysna advice office received an award for excellence in consumer protection for their work on debt traps and micro-lending. Following their campaign, the Department of Trade and Industry was compelled to pass measures protecting consumers, proving right the Ethiopian proverb, "When enough spiders' webs unite, they can tie down a lion."

One area that continued to be a struggle was pension payouts – a story of bungled administration for many years. Post-1994 the situation became even more dire and the advice office became increasingly drawn into this struggle. I spent many days visiting the social security office in Bisho trying to untangle individual pension problems, and talked to a succession of MECs for welfare. One day as one of them opened a bulging cupboard, an avalanche of cardboard files and papers cascaded to the floor. It was clear that there was no prospect of discovering individual records in that mess. In frustration and embarrassment she shouted at me that I had "too many accusations!"

We were fortunate to have the Grahamstown Legal Resources Centre as our great ally in the pensions struggle. The director accompanied two of us from the Sash office to meet with the Public Protector, Selby Baqwa, in Pretoria in July 1997. We struggled for 16 months to get access to him, and it was only when we enlisted the help of Carmel Rickard of the *Sunday Times* that we finally got our interview. Armed with information from our monitoring of pension pay points and social security offices, we unloaded our problems on the Protector's desk. We told him of long delays in the processing of applications for social grants, and lack of feedback on the progress of applications. Our researchers had shown that the average waiting period after application was 15 months or more. We quoted again the story that had received widespread press coverage, of 800 grant applications dumped outside a pension office, some having been used as toilet paper. One man's affidavit described a typical scene at an East Cape pension payout point: "Officials arrive late, about 11am or 12 noon, anytime they choose. The officials take out two chairs. Then the computer dies down. They tell the people to go home. The same the next day. At one point they announce that the money is finished." Not for nothing were cartoonists referring to the Eastern Cape as the Province of Chaotica. The devolution of power to this province had not been to the benefit of the people.

The Public Protector heard us out and promised to visit the province, which he eventually did. In the meantime the Legal Resources Centre began to take batches of delayed pension applications to court, with considerable success. We also managed to get some good media publicity. I had an article published in the *Mail and Guardian*, in which I accused the Eastern Cape government of laying on road shows like Roman circuses to divert the populace's attention from the issues of the day. This remark had an interesting echo in a later TV show in which I participated.

The programme *Two Ways* gave studio audiences the opportunity to ask questions of a panel on a selected topic. On November 1998, I participated in one on pensions. My fellow panelists were a representative of the Disabled Persons Association and the Minister of Social Welfare Geraldine Fraser-Moleketi, to whom I had referred in a letter to the *Business Day* as "the young minister". She had clearly taken exception to this, for while we were being made up, with a communal powder puff, she accused me of having been patronising. "But Geraldine," I retorted, "I was appealing to you as a sister in the struggle!" I don't believe she was mollified. During the programme I thought her handling of questions was bright and articulate, but hard, even ruthless. No-one who saw her in action that day would have described her as "the young minister" – or would have had the gall to claim her as a sister!

The questions from the studio audience were all too familiar to anyone involved in the pension crisis and, although usually thinking on my feet was not a strength, I did not find it difficult to respond. A member of the audience who had misunderstood my *Mail & Guardian* piece complained that to his knowledge not a single circus laid on by the government had passed his way. But the best moment came when a disability grant holder stepped forward, waving his identity book, quoting his number, shouting at the minister and asking her why his grant had been stopped. It was a dramatic micro-demonstration of widespread grassroots distress.

In 1999, after five years in the Black Sash advice office, I began to realise that it was time to retire from the fray. I still felt a strong passion for the work but I could tell that the colour of my skin, the manner of my speech and everything about my image was no longer right for leading the advice office into the future. My much younger colleagues, under the leadership of Jonathan

Walton, were more than able to continue the work. So with the millennium approaching, our first grandchild on the way and Malvern's own retirement coming into view, I took my leave, knowing that I would continue to work for the community but in other ways and perhaps at a gentler pace. We were also keen to travel more widely than we had done in the past. As a little girl I used to lug the heavy atlas out of my father's glass-fronted bookcase and gaze at the maps, promising myself that I would go to all sorts of exotic places. It was 1996 before I visited India with two friends, and now China and Nepal were beckoning.

Actually, I was rather nervous about retirement, worrying that I might be sidelined and have little to do. As it turned out I quickly found myself busy again. I realised that my expertise was still of some use when organisations like the Legal Resources Centre and the Public Service Accountability Monitor called on my help. And when the Friends of the Library asked me to sit on their committee I found my new passion. I was pleased to throw myself into this new task. How else would I ever have met the Fingo Village Revolutionaries, a group of gentle Rastafarians who worked in the Fingo township library promoting perhaps the one thing our society needed most – books, reading and knowledge.

At home

"Come on, family, how shall we celebrate the millennium?" I asked at dinner one evening early in 1999. Fortunately only our youngest, Lucy, was still at home and numbers around the dinner table no longer reached the critical mass for producing a collective groan. Anna was married and living in London while Matthew and Charlotte were both working in Cape Town. Lucy entered into the spirit of the ensuing brainstorm and it was she who said, with a Shakespearian flourish, "Let's put a girdle round the earth." And so we came up with the idea of a walk around the globe, or at least a global walk, in which we would get our friends in various parts of the world to participate. Malvern may have groaned inwardly, but he responded with his usual amusement, "I thought you were retiring this year, my dear."

Malvern and our children were not the only ones who trembled slightly at my enthusiasms. When I retired from the advice office my friends and colleagues presented me with a book of tributes in which several of them alluded to the rather intimidating demands I apparently made. Sheena Duncan described a daily ream of fax paper curling onto her floor, followed by my phone call to check whether she'd got it and what she thought of it. She claimed she was often too afraid to confess she'd not read it yet. Someone else suggested that I'd been born draped in a sash and wielding a chairperson's gavel! I know that I sometimes exasperated people by "chairing" a committee when I was not in the chair, making another colleague describe me as "a good chairperson but a demon of an ex-chairperson". Is this what my friends in the East London advice office meant when one of them wrote in a card, "Before you retire give us tips, how did you manage to be one of the more arrogant women but being cool and calm most times"? I had always been inspired by the Tibetan proverb, "Better to live one day as a tiger than a thousand years as a sheep", and if living as a tiger meant *being* a bit of a tiger then so be it. For the most part my colleagues were tigers themselves, so I took with a pinch of salt the cartoon they had drawn of me jogging along in my sash (though actually jogging is something no one would ever have seen me doing), with a phalanx of panting and exhausted Sashers following in my wake. Funniest of all is a cartoon (adapted from a UNESCO cartoon in the Sash magazine of March 1988) of me as a dungareed child bawling slogans like "freedom", "justice" and "peace" while my parents cower on a couch wondering, "What are we going to do with her when she grows up?" My Grahamstown friends, who had not known my parents, could not have realised how accurately they were portraying them. And the cartoonist's solution to my parents' predicament? "Sending her to Africa seemed the only answer!"

Whenever I was asked to list my favourite things I always said that one of them was going downhill really fast on a bicycle. I suppose that is how I lived. But I also always listed quieter pleasures like nude bathing and eating Greek yoghurt with honey.

In the course of 1999 Malvern and I planned the millennium hike we had hatched with Lucy round our dinner table that night. We contacted friends around the world inviting them to do a hike as near to New Year's day as possible in the hope that, at 10 kilometres per hiker, we could accumulate a total of 1 000 km. We encouraged people to choose a historically significant destination, to send a brief record of their group's effort, and to mark the occasion with a donation to a charity of their choice. We were amazed by the response. Photographs and stories came in from around the globe. Great Britain had the most representatives and their walks ranged from country rambles with small family groups to a 40-strong multigenerational party tramping over the Cotswolds; from a rain-soaked walk along the Thames in London to a march across the bogs and crags of north-west Scotland to find the remains of a crashed World

War II plane. In America friends did the Pacific Crest Trail and in Australia a party of 13 walked from Spit Bridge to Reef Beach along the north of Sydney harbour. David Woods, the Rhodes vice chancellor at the time, and his wife, Charlotte, walked in the Ithala Game Reserve and into the foothills of Swaziland. Val and Trevor Letcher, whose family had tolled the Grahamstown cathedral bells during political protests of yore, walked in Namibia, while our own party strode along the Eastern Cape beach from Riet River to the Three Sisters. I enjoyed the walk with old friends like Jackie Cock, Kathy Satchwell and Julia and Chris Mann, but our record of the day shows a photograph of Malvern reluctantly holding the fort at home, following a neck operation. A grand total of 1 234 km was walked "around the earth" on or around 1 January 2000.

Over the years our house hosted endless meetings, many parties and much fun, and the album that records most of these is our visitors' book. To begin with it reflects Malvern's political aspirations in the Progressive Party. Joyce and Colin Eglin, Alex and Jenny Boraine and Helen Suzman all stayed with us in those early days, when the talk was of election campaigns and anti-apartheid strategies. Then there were the writers and academics like Noni Jabavu visiting from Nairobi, Es'kia Mphahlele and Rob Amato. One of our visitors wrote down this definition of a university from the American poet, Robert Hillyer:

> Where scholars prepare other scholars, not for life,
> but for gaudy footnotes and a threadbare wife.

This was certainly apt for our struggles on an academic salary, but also for Malvern's battle to find time for writing and keeping up with trends in literary thinking. At first the academic visitors from abroad were few and far between, owing to the boycott of South Africa in the 1970s and 1980s. However, Lionel Knights and Muriel Bradbrook of Cambridge, both well-known scholars, did visit and we felt fortunate to have contact with such great minds during a time of increasing isolation. The poet Sydney Clouts lived next door for a while. He was often caught up in enthusiastic bursts of emotion and once whirled me down the street at night saying, "Grahamstown is just like Paris!" I must say I failed to see the similarity.

From the 1980s onward the visitors' book begins to reflect the growing number of people visiting from abroad on anti-apartheid business: Oxfam and Amnesty International workers, British MPs and members of embassies, representatives of churches in Scandinavia and Germany. And as the new era dawned, more local figures too. Perhaps most notable of these was Frene Ginwala, who came in 1990. The Black Sash hosted her at a meeting in the office after which we brought her home for supper. A peculiar meeting occurred in our living room later that evening when a local ANC activist arrived in her nightdress to meet with Frene. It had clearly been past her bedtime when she received the call delegating her to represent the local movement. I was impressed again, as I had been in Harare, by Frene Ginwala's incisive mind and I was not surprised when she was later appointed the Speaker of South Africa's first democratic parliament.

In 2002 the visitors' book reflects a glorious week in our lives – the visit of Marie and Seamus Heaney. Malvern spent many years teaching and admiring the work of this great poet, and to mark Malvern's retirement a colleague arranged to bring Heaney to Grahamstown for a week. It was an imaginative and bold plan. As a Nobel laureate Heaney was much in demand all over the world and we really didn't think he would come, but Wendy Jacobson is nothing but determined. As Marie later said, "I told Seamus this Wendy means business. You'd better go." In the event the town rose to the occasion, the university took the opportunity of holding an extraordinary graduation ceremony to bestow an honorary doctorate on him, and we made two wonderful new friends. The visit was a cultural feast and everything worked with clockwork precision – down to a roaring salute, as though on cue, from a lion when the Heaneys visited in the local Shamwari Game Reserve.

Most memorable was a poetry reading in the cathedral, preceded by a procession from the Drostdy Arch. Walking down High Street amidst this cheerful crowd of students, local poets and academics, I recalled the many political marches that had taken place down this same street, and as we entered the cathedral I thought how fitting that the building that had offered shelter to so many of our angry and anxious protests in the past should tonight be the venue of such a joyous occasion. Seamus and Marie were not the only two people who were bowled over by what awaited them inside the cathedral. Never in our wildest dreams had Wendy, Malvern or I thought that the cathedral would be full to overflowing for a poetry reading! People were crammed on chancel steps and all along the aisles. Candlelight flickered on the grey stone walls. The shouts of a praise poet lifted the roof as he led Malvern and Seamus to the front. And then it was a heart-stopping moment when the great poet started to read. "Between my finger and my thumb," he read, "the squat pen rests, snug as a gun." We were all entranced but none so much as Malvern. He was delighted and humbled by the entire visit and the event in the cathedral was an unforgettable highlight of his career. Malvern had succeeded Guy Butler as head of the English department at Rhodes in 1979. He'd led the department through the era of post-colonial studies while continuing his own teaching and research. Now, the position of Emeritus Professor would give him the opportunity to concentrate on his writing.

One of the meetings frequently hosted in our living room, over a period of more than 40 years, was a monthly gathering of 20 women friends called, accurately if prosaically, the Third Thursday Essay Group. On arriving in Grahamstown in 1966 and feeling socially adrift, I'd begun to search for friends with like minds. One of the activities that had stimulated me and made me feel so much more at home during our brief stay in the United States had been a women's group called Friends in Council. It had its roots in 19th century Kansan life, when a church minister's wife had decided that the ladies of the congregation needed "improving". Each month she'd set an essay topic and the group would get together to read their various offerings, which she then critiqued. Over the years the nature of the group evolved until, by the time we arrived in Lawrence, members no longer had any specific church affiliation and they were taking turns to write essays for the monthly gatherings. My good friend Betsy Bell was a member and took me along to meetings. Fortunately for me the topic that year was 19th century American literature, so I learnt a great deal.

Asking around about anything similar in Grahamstown, I discovered that a newfound friend, Betty Davenport, had previously belonged to such a group in Cape Town. Together with Shirley Maclennan we decided to launch one and, rather gingerly at first, started inviting women we thought might be interested. At a foundation meeting squashed into our temporary flat, Grahamstown's answer to Friends in Council was born. More than four decades later my living room continued to take its turn at hosting these meetings. Amidst the hectic commitments of my working life, the essay group was a date I seldom missed and always looked forward to. Apart from mental stimulation and the company of friends it offered welcome respite from the crises and conflicts that many of us dealt with daily, and it was no surprise that we seldom if ever chose local or socio-political themes to discuss.

When the essay group was joined in the late 1990s by a member who farmed in the Bedford district and arrived at meetings in her double-cab truck, the club started having annual picnics in the Baviaans valley north of Bedford. Gill Pringle would lay on a spread under a thorn tree, complete with champagne and balloons, and we would laze on rugs in the shade and listen to readings on a theme we had chosen for the day. Occasionally conditions were conducive to nude bathing in the Baviaans stream, but on other occasions severe drought confined us to the garden around the farmhouse.

Spending time with friends was important to me, but of course there were those I was unable to see regularly, such as Caroline Starling, my great university friend and bridesmaid, and so letter writing became our form of communication. How I rejoiced over the years at the sight of Caroline's regulation

Royal Mail envelopes with their Par Avion stickers, and how I enjoyed replying to them! In the early years especially, I valued my various correspondences enormously. Copious letters to and from friends, most of them in England but several scattered around the world, allowed me to gain perspective on my life and the events going on around me. They were windows onto other worlds, with views that helped keep me sane, and at the same time they provided me with a kind of vicarious window onto my own life. Through them I could always feel at my back the wonderful support of an interested and caring network of friends.

Besides the constant stream of friends and colleagues, our house in time became home to Grahamstown's Quaker meetings. The book-lined room which opened onto the garden had first been a bedroom and playroom. With a new ceiling and another set of French doors it later became known as the garden room, and now it became the meeting room. Here, away from the road, one could meditate in quiet, interrupted only by the sound of oriole or pigeon or cicada. The British travel writer Freya Stark once said that old age comes most gently to those who have doorways into an abstract world. After a lifetime of being too busy for much contemplation, such a doorway eventually opened to me in the old library of Pembroke College, during a sabbatical leave in Cambridge.

My great-aunt Elsie, who had been a Quaker, had left an abiding impression on me, but we'd never talked about her faith and in the family it had been alluded to more as an intellectual adventure than a spiritual conviction. At university, a boyfriend had introduced me to the principles of pacifism and during the holidays in Cornwall, where my parents then lived, I went down steep country lanes to a thatched Meeting House with cool, whitewashed walls that rejoiced in the name of Come to Good. Later still, when we came to Grahamstown, I attended some meetings, but my growing family claimed my attention and my attendance soon petered out. Then while on leave with Malvern in Cambridge in 1993, I cycled each Sunday morning to Pembroke College where, in the peace of a paneled room that had been a library for generations of students, the Cambridge Friends encouraged my bumbling efforts on a new journey of faith.

In all the turmoil of my life in South Africa, there had been a part of me that longed for stillness. In my initial alienation I had rushed to the Anglican Church, finding in its building and familiar services something that quenched my homesickness. But I was annoyed by its hierarchies and often felt its members in general acquiesced too easily to apartheid. The Quakers, by contrast, had a consistent heritage of humanitarianism here and elsewhere, and the democracy of their church governance appealed to me. Once I'd become a regular member I was happy that our house could host this very different kind of gathering, in the silence of which I was beginning to learn to be still.

One of the best-kept secrets of our Market Street house was its garden. Because the house faced straight onto the street, without a drive or front area, no one expected the spacious, tree-filled back garden. When we first moved in I cultivated the friendship of the head gardener at the university who on occasion loaded my car with saplings and plants, saying, "I don't think the vice chancellor's garden will miss these." Over the years the trees grew, and especially in the early summer they soared up into a green canopy of oak, erythrina, chestnut, mulberry, yellowwood and Cape lilac. There was a long stretch of grass on which the children pitched tents, learnt to ride bikes and played badminton, and in time it would provide space for eight grandchildren to play in. It was definitely a garden for parties, of which there were many, especially in the summertime, but mostly it was our refuge from the outside world. Some time after the children had all left home, Malvern wrote the poem *Aerial Photography*:

> The lawn is silent now
> Screened by trees
> No older than the children
> Who used to fill each summer
> With their tents and games and laughter.

Turning green by solar clockwork,
They can no more be seen
From my study window:
The rich compost of soil and sun
Ensures that in their genes
The life of youth will turn again,
And again, shut off from ageing eyes
Which search in vain
For the aerial photograph
Of childhood's shadow
Impressed forever on the grass.

When I was a child I spent a lot of time cutting out pictures from magazines of houses and gardens – usually manor houses with extensive lawns – and then I would fantasise about the rich husband I would have and the many children who would complete the romance. Feminism and political struggles were unknown concepts to a middle-class English girl. My mother never had a career and had very little experience outside the home. She did encourage me to train for something, but only "to fall back on", and though my friends and I all started out on careers, our eyes were really on marriage. To marry and be supported by one's husband was still the expectation. None of our daughters, I am pleased to say, has thought of her career as an insurance policy only.

The world has changed. And so did my life, from fantasies and dreams of a romantic idyll to a reality I could not have imagined. For my 70th birthday the family gave me a garden swing seat. As a child I'd had to swing in other people's gardens as all we had was a rather uncomfortable hammock slung between two sycamores, which tipped at unexpected moments. I'd always wanted a swing of my own. Reclining in it now, the warm sun on my legs and a book open beside me, I recall my expectation that Malvern and I would ultimately park our caravan in the English countryside. Two of our four children, like swallows, have flown north. I suppose I will always continue to feel that pull. But it's nostalgia, not regret.

When I think back to the child I was, and the home and country I grew up in, I have to pinch myself. Was that me? Has this been my life? By South African standards my life has not been remarkable. My story is not one of suffering or heroic deeds, but the simple record of one woman's life in a provincial town on an extraordinary frontier. Against all my early expectations I've become completely absorbed in this very strange society – and that has made all the difference.

CPSIA information can be obtained at www.ICGtesting.com
Printed in the USA
BVOW07s1423121214

379161BV00003B/128/P